DUNES REVIEW

NO A.I. TRAINING: Without in any way limiting the authors' and publisher's exclusive rights under copyright, any use of this publication to "train" generative artificial intelligence (AI) technologies to generate text is expressly prohibited. The publisher reserves all rights to license uses of this work for generative AI training and development of machine learning language models.

EDITORIAL BOARD

SENIOR EDITORS Teresa Scollon
  Jennifer Yeatts

EDITOR Kelli Fitzpatrick

DIGITAL EDITOR Yvonne Stephens

READERS Chris Giroux
  John Mauk
  Sara Maurer
  Anne-Marie Oomen

FOUNDING EDITOR Anne-Marie Oomen

Thank you to this issue's Patrons:
Bronwyn Jones
Anne-Marie Oomen
Joan Richmond
Phillip Sterling
In Memory of John Pahl

COVER IMAGE: "Catskill Deer Skull Reflection" by Tyler Franz, photography. Image courtesy of the artist.

DUNES REVIEW
VOLUME 29 ISSUE 1
SPRING/SUMMER 2025

CONTENTS

viii	EDITORIAL	Land Acknowledgement
	TYLER FRANZ	Cover Artist's Statement
1	TERESA SCOLLON	
	JENNIFER YEATTS	Editors' Notes
3	MICHAEL MARK	In the Subway
4	JEFF KASS	Small Rise
6	ROBERT FANNING	*GRUNNVATN* // GROUNDWATER
7	DEBORAH ALLBRITAIN	There is Nothing Left to Know
8	DAN GERBER	After a Long Time Away
9	KEITH TAYLOR	Going Under
10	NANCY SQUIRES	The Garden
11	MARY JO FIRTH GILLETT	Wild Solitude
12	PHILLIP STERLING	The Miracle of Perspective
13	DAN GERBER	Forest
14	KEITH TAYLOR	Implacable
15	ALICE HAINES	Red Osier
16	SHUTTA CRUM	The Revelation of the Wood
17	CLAIRE HELAKOSKI	Baby Blues [CNF]
19	DAVID JAMES	Finding Your Place in the World
20	JULIE BONNER WILLIAMS	Spinners
21	COLLEEN ALLES	Physics
24	JACK RIDL	Feeding the Fish

25	Richard Hoffman	From an Adirondack Chair
26	Michael Mark	Cleaning the Backyard Furniture
27	David Hardin	Land Ho ^{CNF}
33	Andrew Collard	Autotopia
34	Ephraim Scott Sommers	Ode to This, Us on a Winter Day, Staring out the Window at the New World
36	Monica Finger	Bug Jar
38	Andrew Jeter	The Conceit
39	Brian Builta	October 10
40	B.A. Van Sise	San Juan
41	Karly Vance	Tessellation
42	Katherine Roth	The Feather of a Gull
43	Kara Penn	Murder of Crows
44	Elizabeth Kerlikowse	Dementia and the Wild Man ^{CNF}
47	Meghan Sterling	Winter is an Unreliable Narrator
48	Kenton K. Yee	Moon Pie Lover
49	Anita Hunt	Canning Sunlight
50	Ellen Stone	Quart Mason Jars
51	April Yu	Solstice ^F
57	Jason Gordy Walker	Father to Son
58	Roger D'Agostin	Plumbing ^F
62	LeAnn Peterson	Love and Knitting ^{CNF}
64	Robert Fanning	*JARÐHITI* // GEOTHERMAL
65	Mary Dean Lee	Taste of You
66	Monica Rico	Rounding Cape Horn
67	B.A. Van Sise	Labor Day, Brooklyn
69	B.A. Van Sise	Artifact
70	John Flesher	Know When to Run ^{CNF}
77	Phillip Sterling	The Miracle of Higher Elevations
78	Ryan McCarty	Never Asking
79	Patricia Clark	One Sister Said to the Other "I Have Sad News"
80	Monica Rico	Autopilot
82	Julia Bedell	To Be One of the Birds ^F
90	Sheena M. Carey	Kintsugi

91	Russ Capaldi	Lighter Things
93	Devin Wilson	Crickets
94		Contributor Bios
100		Staff Bios
104		Submission Guidelines
105		Call for Members and Patrons

f = Fiction
cnf = Creative NonFiction

Land Acknowledgement

Dunes Review is published on the traditional lands of the Grand Traverse Band of Ottawa and Chippewa Indians. It is important to understand the long-standing history that has brought us to reside on the land, and to seek to understand our place within that history. We give honor to the Anishinaabe people for their continual contributions to the land and society.

Cover Artist's Statement

My work is heartfelt, emotional, and heavily influenced by my love of black and white photography. Preserving moments in an image is my passion and nature is my happy place. Combine the two, and that is where I feel most at peace. There is something really special about capturing the human spirit in a photograph, doing what you love most with those who are dear to you. I'm here for the artists, the dreamers, the lovers, and for those who walk through life leading with their hearts. This life is so beautiful and I absolutely love capturing humans doing what makes them happy. Photography is a way of feeling, of touching, of loving. We were put on this earth to inspire one another through respect and compassion.

—*Tyler Franz*

Editors' Notes

You are reading this issue of *Dunes Review* because it is paid for by your Michigan Writers membership fees. The costs of printing, shipping, launch readings, and a Submittable subscription are our largest expenses. The cover artists generously donate the use of their work. Once in a while we run into a jam and hire someone to help with layout. Otherwise, all of the human effort that goes into this journal is volunteered. Because of all this, we are somewhat insulated by the funding crisis that is wiping out arts organizations right now. The Michigan Humanities website includes a page for Poetry Out Loud, a national program in which my high school students have participated for several years and which now bears this message: "The Department of Government Efficiency (DOGE) has terminated all funding to humanities councils. Therefore, all programs and grants are currently suspended." Our local treasure, the Dennos Museum, is scrambling to replace federal funding in order to continue its programs. It's no secret that many Michigan Writers members are of a certain age, with the resources to help to support a literary community. We need each other, plain and simple, and we know it. Thank you so much. And now: what about our kids? Arts education and support is an important part of developing young people. Isn't one measure of a civilization's worth how it provides for its young?

— *Teresa Scollon*

It amazes me every single time: the way, when we begin arranging and rearranging them, re-reading for the twelfth time, the individual pieces we select start new conversations among themselves. Over the first few pages of this issue, we travel from a subway car to a morning bike commute, each scene oozing with relatable human angst. Then several pages of poets—who must be in cahoots as far as I can tell—pull us along into fields of tall grasses that might also be oceans or rivers but are more likely just the perfect metaphor for the contoured paths we all wander, whether by navigating actual boats or simply by putting one foot in front of the other, again and again.

That's what good writing does, doesn't it? Pulls us inside, guides us along, tugs on the threads of shared human experience and stitches us together. Thanks for being here for this particular journey, for stepping into this little book along with the rest of us.

— *Jennifer Yeatts*

Michael Mark
IN THE SUBWAY

Would you look at my wound? I asked
the person sitting next to me. (I won't
describe them for two reasons.) They said
they're not a doctor. I was concerned
they would change seats or get off the next
stop so right then I showed them my wound
and to anyone close enough to see. It's deep
and wide and raw and I'm never without it but
people don't look or they pretend they don't
notice. I said, before this person said anything,
you don't have to say anything, in fact, don't.
Don't diagnose or prescribe treatment or
presume how it got so ugly. Above all, please
don't cry. Just witness, validate the existence
of my wound. But they did cry. And their wound
bled and oozed, like a child collapsing in relief,
all over the train.

Jeff Kass
SMALL RISE

Sometimes it rains on the way
to the gym. Sometimes construction
cones hog the bike lane. Sometimes
a passenger opens a car door and clocks
me in the shins. Okay, that happened

only once.

I'll admit it, I'm not always
in a stellar mood at six-fifteen
in the morning, especially if
my soaked clothes stick

to my skin like wax and rain
spits into my face and, look,
some days I don't particularly
lust to be at work where my first
words to students inevitably will
be *okay, that's the bell, get the fish
hooks out the sides of your heads,
have your phones navigate immediately
to your backpacks*, but roughly a half
mile from the gym, about a hundred
yards after climbing the second
biggest hill on the ride and about
thirty yards before crossing
the somewhat rickety bridge
over the highway, the bike path
dips sharply and no streetlights
illumine the darkness and I gain
speed which isn't exactly scary
but also reminds me how little
control I have over any damn
thing in my life, and just when
I could conceivably panic and/or,
if I were a more responsible person,

pump the brakes to slow down, the dip
recedes like a tide, or a migraine,

and I am cradled by a barely
perceptible rise in the path
that tenderly stalls the bike's
careen and my lungs inflate
as if I have inherited the sky-
blue chest of a sing-songy
Smurf, or become a balloon
lofting free from the cling
of a tree, and I would be remiss
if I didn't say, every day, this
small geography saves me.

Robert Fanning
GRUNNVATN // GROUNDWATER

Somewhere along the way your being begins
to wither. Cracked fields, the grasses of your life
hollow. Spiritdry. Landbound. Did you dream it
would be easy leaving your self? In your bones, the sea
becomes memory. The body so easily forgets what
it carries. Well, skáld—find me. All you can't see
nourishes, ever moving. You know the place you're
afraid to stand—for fear of being drawn away?

Begin there.

Deborah Allbritain
THERE IS NOTHING LEFT TO KNOW

My solitude is like the grass — It contains an oarless boat.
A woman passed me on my walk today, nodded as if she understood

all the ways I kept a lid on myself, how at all times I
held the bit between my teeth.

He thought I was asking to feed *off* him when really

I only wanted a sweater, an orchard
tucked inside the sleeves,
two humans worth saving.

When he evaporated for the third time he cast a shadow
down the rest of my life.

It was the last nail that held my heart in place.
How can I explain there is no little rudder, that when

the words come out they sound like something splashing?

Dan Gerber
AFTER A LONG TIME AWAY

He came to a place so far from the sea,
no one knew what an oar was for, where

no rudder had ever come about, and
no one had dreamed of embarking.

A hardwood oar, ash, the kind a slave might
have pulled, in the hull of a Roman galley,

he carried for protection and to salve his
separation from the sea. He dug

a small hole to plant the oar, its high-flown blade
dividing the sun and wind into

shadow and the shelter of deflection, and
with no other purpose there, the oar began to

take on meanings, perhaps to herald a new
planet, or the tidal pull of a distant shore.

Keith Taylor
GOING UNDER

Then, the bird who intends it:
who dives straight down,
head first, disappearing all
together in the watery world
below him: tern falling aware
or not of suffering —
how can we ever know? —
straight from flight to dive to swim
before exploding upward,
sexual and fertile, shaking
off water on the wing, returned
with something silver in his bill.

Nancy Squires
THE GARDEN

You must not set your feet down
in the garden—float
above the beds, the rows

of ruffled lavender, bowing
in sea-breeze, the branches
of small trees reaching

for the sun, knots of mustard yellow
growing on the ground—
but they are colonies

not cabbages and the flash
of canary darting in and out,
flitting frond to frond

has fins. Kick softly,
glide through the grove
in silence while filtered sunlight

casts soft shadow on the sand.
It's against the law to stand
here in the garden; this place

will not bear our weight.

Mary Jo Firth Gillett
WILD SOLITUDE
after Keith Taylor

Once you get past the fishy smell,
   the regularity of waves whooshing
   against the side of the plywood pram —
   gentle waves whispering you are
   more vulnerable than you know —

Once you ease into the quiet tick-tick
   of aloneness — despite how far you are
   from the shore, despite how, as the wind
   picks up, the anchor won't hold —
   how delicious to relax into the drift.

Once you no longer worry about how deep
   it is, how far above the bottom you are,
   there is only the tug of possibility on your line,
   and the gossamer threads of a tiny spider on the reel —
   echoes of the great wilderness inside you.

Phillip Sterling
THE MIRACLE OF PERSPECTIVE

A dull patch of wild ducks do their best to hold water to the river, but morning dissolves them into fog, lifting them from the millpond's reflection like hints of annunciation. The river whispers, mere dribble and ripple of the ducks' faint attempts. Today the fish will sleep late, the sun linger at the windowsill like an indecisive cat. Shall we go out in it? Or shall we stay inside instead, pretend it's a saint's day, fix sticky buns and bacon, maybe grapefruit? What difference would it make? Call it an excuse—the world's impractical futility. Call it another form of splendor.

Dan Gerber
FOREST
Guy de La Valdine, May 8, 1944 — March 31, 2023

Last night I woke in the roaring
dark of a forest I couldn't see, as if

waking in the body of a great beast, breathing,
the creak and groan of a thousand

schooner masts aching at their stays and
the bright, turpentine, pitch of spruce.

I fell asleep here in the late afternoon, after
trudging a mile up from the creek, light

only a memory now, save a few scattered
stars, straight overhead, fragments of a constellation

unknown among the obfuscating fir crowns,
the only light to confirm I still have eyes.

Death is not the great leap you think it is,
unless you choose to leap.

Do you remember your birth that way? If you
are reading this, you are somewhere in between,

in a forest of fading and renewing life,
or maybe in a desert, waiting. We

cannot actually see a star. We see its history still
trailing our way and are persuaded we exist

to find ourselves alive here
and perceive it.

Keith Taylor
IMPLACABLE

> *... the old/Implacable arrogance ...*
> — Robinson Jeffers, "Hurt Hawks"

Squirrels scatter
when the red-tailed hawk
flies in from the neighbor's birch
to the black oak
outside my study window.

Finches and juncos hide
in brush piles
but her yellow eyes
look past the minor politics
of small birds.

She sees me, back-lit,
looking out at her,
but she doesn't care.

Even when she ruffles
her soft breast feathers and preens,
she displays sharp places —
her curved, flesh-ripping beak,
the terrible talons
(ready to impale)
that she lifts to scratch
gently
the underside of her wings.

Alice Haines
RED OSIER

> *A stitch in time saves...*
> —Proverb

It's a bush of a bush: stalks cigar-thick
and greening, maroon skin barely flushed,
haloed with air-tickling twigs, dense
within. Come leaf-out it'll shade
the rest. Cutting out sticks in time
may save the lowbush blueberries
behind and their leaves of fall scarlet.

Rather than cut to ground, I'm thinning,
trying to hoard some muted red
since there's not one yellow crocus up
yet. I clip out wands, pick at them
like misplaced stitches in a seam —
in time create a meager creature
topped with fuzz, find an eclectic,

puzzled topiary. Wind
writhes and tangles my brittle hair
and the dangling threads of my worn jacket.
Face winter-pale, eyes creased, my mouth.
is held within parenthesis.
Life has certainly taken a stitch
in time — pleated the blue horizon.

And here I am, kneeling to a bush.

Shutta Crum
THE REVELATION OF THE WOOD

scar tissue or malignant growth —
a burl is an ugly thing
lumpy, hard, and harvested in early winter
from the smooth bole of birch, or elm

but when cut, gouged out
and the puckered bark abraded
it becomes something holy
in calloused hands

pop-veined and stained by labor
my father's hands lift, smooth, oil,
reveal the communion
of light and wood

even when the grain
has grown wildly impulsive
and as undisciplined as the child by his side
everything spirals heavenward

Claire Helakoski
BABY BLUES

The moon watched as I held you close, kissed your head, soft and sweet-smelling, in the dark aloneness, like every mother through history who has sat in the night, holding her baby, whispering *I love you*, and crying tears of exhaustion, emotion, overwhelm. Blues, they call it, baby blues.

And it is blue in these hours of darkness, snow shadows stretching blue, and your veins in your tiny forehead are blue, the blanket I cover you with in sunlight hours has blue stars on it, but blue is not the color of my feelings. Black despair and unending night, dragged up by the hair from sleep like I'm drowning, waterboarded, wishing to stay beneath the surface and dream. These days are black as cast iron, black as the smoke from my mother's homemade roux, black like a sky with no stars even though they must be out there because they exist even in the daylight, even when you cannot see them—holes of light in the universe.

Like your eyes, which are blue, which someone tells me look like a galaxy. I am new to the weight of a strange atmosphere on this planet of motherhood where I can't breathe. Can you breathe? I listen as your lungs shudder at night and hold, hold, wait to hear a rhythm, relax once your small chest rises evenly. The gravity here is so dense I can barely move, barely make food, take a shower, get up off the bed or couch. I only see the walls of my room, the shadow of a tree. Where is my ability to feel joy? Has all of it been soaked up into you, sleeping being who needs and needs? Or perhaps my heavier body, pulled down and down, can no longer bounce happiness through itself. My atoms are too sluggish, unable to vibrate at the frequency of joy. I feel as though I have changed forms, or that the lifeform I was will not survive here, and I'm losing the parts that made me who I was.

I'm supposed to be happy with my baby. And when you smile, I smile. And I still picture your tiny perfect face, etching it again and again into my mind until I know you, before I fall asleep. But I also can't bear another moment of this. And I can't bear to be away from you. This blueness has permeated everything I see—a filter I can't seem to take off my eyes, goggles I need or otherwise be blind on this planet of clouds, this planet where all I see are the needs of others piling thicker and thicker like smog. There's a name for this: depression.

And later, I will see it for what it is and know there could have been a different kind of healing for me. And later, I will know that there is an end to the fog, that the light will cut through and let me see again. But then, I had to find a different way out. Me and a flashlight, crawling up a mountain I couldn't see the top of, didn't know if I'd ever reach, or what the view might be like from here.

    One day, I go for a drive and see color: yellow, green, pink. The red buds' rosy joy has sprung from new branches, birds sing, the sun feels warm against my face. I roll the window down to feel it more fully, cupping my chin in its hands like a mother welcoming a child home, hungry for the lost shape of their face. And this is the first day—weeks after they said it would arrive, after equinox, after the birth of a change, of continued rotation, of shift—this is the first day of spring.

David James
FINDING YOUR PLACE IN THE WORLD
(my Jack Ridl poem)

If you add hope and prayer
to even an ounce of faith
and then mix forgiveness with mercy,
you can drink
from the cup of living.
You'll be able to see
miracles—that hawk up there
gliding on a current, the green buds
opening in the maple, a bright planet
glowing near the bottom
of the western sky.

If you take your time and subtract
the daily worries that tear
at your fingertips, you can enter
that space where nothing matters
except this breath, this music,
the face of your lover
reading beside you
in her favorite chair.

Julie Bonner Williams
SPINNERS

for Jack and Julie Ridl

Upstairs

she is an arachnid, goddess
of the loom, spun fibers
passing between her fingertips
Teak basket beside her cradles
laps of airy weaving, each
strand a line, the lines a stanza
cadence borne of weaver's fingers

Downstairs

He is a monk, scribe with
fingers stained blue
moving ink across the page
Binding at his elbow
grasps orphan page: each
line a strand, each strand a fabric
tapestry borne of poet's hand

Colleen Alles
PHYSICS

I'm meant to close
the curtains in our bedroom
      at night, but

      more than once, I've let
the soft fabric spool
         in both hands
when I spy them —

the neighbors —

through
their big kitchen window.

My eyes are
     on their bodies
        turning toward one another
then away;

they rotate and revolve
in the lit-up room —

     planets orbiting
     their kitchen
     island. The wide

swing of the fridge door,
     Rachel shuffling a pot
     by the handle
     from one palm to her other, smiling.

I imagine she's saying
        to Phil

something mundane,
     like I bought you beer today, or

         something insane,
         like do you realize we've been married
         longer than we haven't?

         This far away, I can
         have them say
anything. Maybe

         she's asking

         about gravity: where we'd be
                  without its thick blanket
                           holding us
                  to the Earth. He's nodding — yes,

         without gravity, we'd float
away — and his hands go

         in the air, and Rachel
                  nods too — but

         what about friction? she asks.
         Without friction we'd slide

endlessly

         past one another, forever
         and

right then
         I'm some kind of God
         in the back
         of my bedroom

because he closes
         the distance between them
                  and wraps Rachel in a hug

                  and I know it's because

22

        I've made them talk about
        gravity and friction — such simple,
        invisible miracles

that when I see Rachel
    the next morning
        walking her dog, I almost
            say something

about how nice it is
        they've had each other
           for so long
                to hold onto.

Jack Ridl
FEEDING THE FISH

When my wife gets to the end
of the cobbled together dock,
the fish, mostly bluegill—blue
centered on each side, you know,
and with them often a half dozen
largemouth come and form a
flotilla as she balances and
tosses oatmeal and tiny
marbles of what the owner
of the local family-owned
Fish and Farm assured her
is good for the fish, that they
love the flavor we can't taste.
Our dog, Smug, sits beside her,
face focused on the sparkling fins.
After they've taken all they can
hold, they still eat, often spitting
out two pellets at once. Smug
then jumps into the shallow
believing he can catch one
The fish, untroubled, keep
trying to swallow, keep diving
and rising for what's still floating.
Then several tiny heads show above
the pond's shadowed surface. Turtles.
They snatch what's left, drop down, rise,
drop, rise. My wife stands, watches
and smiles, then starts singing to them
just as she did last evening and the
evening before and will again tomorrow.

Richard Hoffman
FROM AN ADIRONDACK CHAIR

I watched the changing shadows
of clouds the breadth of a reverie
that spanned half a century
moving across green mountains

the scent of mud and grass and
clover just past its bloom joined
in a certain way will always be-
come what I remembered then

you next to me eyes closed face
toward the sun serene as shadows
moved across us very fast the way
our lives were gathering speed

Michael Mark
CLEANING THE BACKYARD FURNITURE

I thought it would last longer - the *natural*
      Indonesian luster. Like a luxury
resort you go to, no, I go into debt

to go to, and pretend
      this is how I live all the time, my palms
smoothing the lake-facing

Adirondack's armrests – extravagant grain
      of other people's good fortune.
So when I walked out this morning to my flimsy

dull, sad, worn replicas, I saw my life.
      This is the truth about how it's been going.
My life, I thought. I will wash

and dry and wash again the story all out of me.

David Hardin
LAND, HO

This is an excerpt taken from the forthcoming memoir, Water Finds a Way *(Cornerstone Press), a reflection on the author's relationship with his father, a poor Appalachian immigrant to booming post-war Detroit.*

You can go home again, contrary to Thomas Wolfe, but be prepared for a long drive with few decent rest stops. In the early years, it was eighteen hours over two-lane state and county roads running through small towns scattered like Percocet over the somnolent counterpane of Ohio, winding steadily into rising hopes waiting to be dashed in Kentucky. We would make the trip all in one go, motoring in a madhouse-green 1953 Buick Deluxe Sedan. My father, calling on his long-haul skills, did most of the driving. Sleep came reliably to my insomniac mother only when she was behind the wheel centered nominally between the double yellow line and the guardrail, proverbial abyss rushing by on the right, oncoming trucks bearing down on the left. Turning the wheel over to her would have demanded a leap of faith unavailable to most.

    My father was stingy with intangibles and tended to avoid stepping off into the thin air of faith. He would have had to be nearly comatose with fatigue to let her drive but drive she did when called upon. It's a wonder he managed to close his eyes for more than a heartbeat, let alone the length of a restorative catnap. His nightmares must have rivaled those experienced by returning vets, possibly the worst of his own. We would have been far safer had they balanced me on a stack of phone books, placed a brick on the accelerator, and pointed me toward the Ohio River.

    My father always insisted on early departure, a time of night that, years later during my sorry underage drinking days, I would regard as post-bar, stave-off-a-hangover, greasy spoon time. We covered a lot of ground before the sun came up, driving mostly in the dark. I rode shotgun on my nodding mother's lap; stood on the bench seat between them, taking in the scrolling asphalt; or rolled unrestrained on the backseat like a tin of biscuits. My father relieved himself along the verge on deserted stretches or, having achieved cruising altitude, clenched an empty Nehi bottle between his thighs, squinting through smoke from his Lucky. My mother and I squatted, screened between the open passenger-side doors, flinching at well-timed airhorns, our lungs emptied in the vacuum created by passing trucks.

 Car sickness and I were on a first name basis. Until I was big enough to crank the handle of the rear passenger window, I vomited into the foot well or small ash tray located on the arm rest. Freedom was an open window, contents of my stomach all but sucked out and plastered across the rear fender, my most recent meal sloughing off in the cool night air. My father considered loss of bodily function while on a road trip one of the seven deadly sins, right up there with owning a Chevrolet, keeping an indoor dog, and wasting food, even my mother's incomprehensible cooking.

 Mostly, we rode in near silence, the tip of my father's cigarette a distant red planet reflected in the partially open window next to his face, smoke venting out through the gap like spring melt over a dam. The radio was always on and buzzing, reception spotty. We passed through pockets of music; hillbilly mostly, stretches of sanitized white gospel so denatured of soul as to make the likes of Billy Graham long for a little womp-bomp-a-loom-op. Southern preachers berated us from the darkness. I imagined them leaning red-faced into roadside pulpits, shaking their fists as we blew past, piety and spittle trailing us for miles, radioing ahead to alert the next pompadoured, shit-heel charlatan: *sinners at two o'clock*. My father had little to say, aside from non-sequiturs shared with my mother which I couldn't hear and hadn't much interest in anyway. He hummed, tunelessly, aimlessly. I found it comforting, like hearing the sunrise milkman minus the pleasant tinkling of empty bottles.

The interstate highway system between Detroit and Knoxville, for much of the two decades between the Gulf of Tonkin Incident and Reagan's Morning In America grift, was functionally similar to an otherwise intact gastrointestinal tract with major gaps at key places: Toledo, Dayton, Cincinnati, landslide zones on the Kentucky/Tennessee border, the open air flea market aesthetic of greater Knoxville, and our primary target, a dusky pucker due southeast of Jellico Mountain. My father knew his way around Toledo better than El Greco knew the backstreets of that Ohio city's Spanish eponym. While lesser drivers crossed and recrossed the Maumee again and again, hopelessly lost, seeking re-entry to the interstate, we would be back on the highway at speed, Findley in our rearview mirror, preparing to bid good morning to Wapakoneta.

We had just *run* Toledo, as in, *Buddy, I done run twenty-four over 'turnpike pass mile marker seventeen jus' t' other side of Phlutesburgh—* trucker-speak for *who knows fuck all.*

Fuel stop protocols were sacrosanct; regardless the angle of the needle gauge, our first stop always just south of the Ohio River at the Florence, Kentucky exit. Cessation of forward motion was enough to break the spell and remind us of lunch, still hours distant. Snacks from home were unheard of, especially soda. Anything that required careless noshing or came in a bottle without a nipple, would produce crumbs or risk a catastrophic high fructose corn syrup spill. My father pampered cars the way Bob Wills cradled his fiddle.

Fast food multinationals had yet to discover the commercial value of building restaurants just off the interstate in the blank hinterland between cities. Exit anywhere other than Cincinnati or Lexington, and your choices were Tiny-J's Tay-stee Eetz or a petroleum-scented truck stop where the laminated menus doubled as bathmats in the coin-operated shower stalls around back. My father took offense when anyone complained about eating at the T n'A or Diesel Haus. I wonder whether the offspring of beat cops turn up their noses at the glazed, powdered, and jelly-fills in little Mainstreet doughnut shops.

It was vacation, so hamburgers, fries, and shakes were allowed regardless the time of day. Passing through the border state South, we were regulars at Howard Johnson's and Stuckey's, drawn by fried clams and divinity candy, respectively. My father could tuck into fried clams like a Blue Hen State native. My mother, once she commenced, couldn't resist eating an entire box of gagging-ly sweet divinity candy that no one else in the car, *or anyone in their right mind*, would touch.

Car travel grew only nominally easier with the passage of time. Personal listening devices were years off unless you happened to own a transistor radio or bulky reel-to-reel tape player. AM radio coverage was spotty, and we weren't keen on singing rounds like the Von Trapps. Resonant Paul Harvey might stutter for a moment before lapsing into white noise, time enough for *Jumping Jack Flash* to get a nose under the tent. But before Mick could drone his last, *it's a gas, gas, gas,* Barry Sadler would sputter to life. *Put silver wings on my son's chest.*

Sir, no sir!

One summer, we left the driving to Greyhound. My father couldn't make the trip, for reasons unclear. The official line was, he couldn't get time off work. *Godhelpus*, my mother didn't elect to undertake the drive herself. He was a Teamster who enjoyed decent health benefits, a pension, and paid vacations. He'd driven us every year previous. Possibly, he'd been laid off for a few months over the winter, reducing his vacation time. Had they fought? By this time, they'd been married twelve years. They had a mortgage, two kids, medical bills, the cost of living rising, always rising. My father was pushing forty, victim of an ever-expanding waistline, chronic reflux heartburn, and a dead-end job in which he'd plateaued his first week of work. They argued, but I rarely witnessed harsh words exchanged. The only way to know for certain a disagreement had taken place was to observe anger's gravitational influence on my world. My father's simmering withdrawal. The force with which my mother slammed her coffee cup down on the kitchen table.

What if this were the Big One? Had she packed our winter clothes? Was I to be enrolled in a new school where, to gain the grudging respect of classmates, I would be obliged to engage in fistfights recalling the War Between the Blue and Gray? How often would I be called upon to mount yet another valiant but ineffectual defense, every day another Antietam? My father's presence insured our annual visits would be brief, temporary aberrations of ritualized life up north, his itch to leave palpable from the moment we arrived. Without him, we were no better than disgraced immigrants escaping our failed experiment in New World possibilities, the best we could hope for being a second-hand single-wide in the lower pasture hard by the chicken lot.

My father dropped us at the bus terminal south of Tiger Stadium late one morning, commencing our twenty-plus-hour ordeal. If there were tears, a Rick-and-Ilsa airfield moment, I don't recall. I remember only fragments of the trip accurately, but I'm happy to recount a version that, while just shy of any reasonable margin of truth, captures the spirit of the journey exactly.

If Willie Nelson's first iteration of the *Honeysuckle Rose* had given birth to *Further*, the Blue Bird that ferried the Merry Pranksters to many an acid test, and that tie-dyed legend had mated with a Louisiana State Department of Corrections bus, their offspring would have been our summer chariot to the Southland. The driver fancied himself possessing the Right Stuff in excess: quasi-aviator kit, short sleeve white shirt, clip-on tie, peaked pilot's hat, Pall Malls, and epaulets.

He wore goddam epaulets.

He was a ropy-armed redneck with a pomaded swagger reminiscent of Jerry Lee Lewis's bag man, and he took an immediate shine to my mother. She was young, buxom, alluring in a Hedy Lamar-esque way and, as far as Sam Shephard-cum-Chuck Yeager was concerned, an exotic lady of mystery hot for adventure. That she was traveling with two young boys, the larger, doughier one visibly shaken, as if having just witnessed his first autopsy, seemed not to register. Passengers de-bussed at a succession of increasingly grim rest stops reminiscent of East German border checkpoints manned by jittery adolescent guards high on Dexedrine and black-market be-bop. The fluorescent lights turned our hamburgers a nauseating, spleenish shade of taupe. My mother's lipstick, a lurid carnelian. An unruly lock of hair kept falling over her eye in a way that never happened at home. Since when did she wear stockings with seams? Why hadn't I noticed before that the comforting mole on her upper lip was a wantonly seductive beauty mark?

I couldn't pee to save my soul; relaxing vigilance, even for a few seconds, was much too big a risk for something so transient as mere relief. My bladder would either hold or it wouldn't. Sleep came fitfully and with it, Sam/Chuck in the guise of the Genesis serpent coiled around my mother's milky shoulders like a hissing stole or dozing in the crotch of a strange, anthropomorphic tree, digesting two child-sized lumps, one essentially a five-gallon skin of urine.

It wasn't the bus driver who had me worried, though. What was keeping her from sashaying, ample hips swaying like some translucently pale Ma Rainy, up the aisle to straddle the wiry little peckerwood, take the wheel while he stomped blindly on the gas, and hijack the hound to Reno? Surely my father, if he were there, would have shoved those epaulets where the sun not only didn't shine, but would never emerge from behind a dark cloud of impotent rage. But he was on the road in West Virginia or Pennsylvania—working the Peruvian guano mines, for all I knew. It was all up to me, so I squared my shoulders and did what I did best; worried myself constipated. I would spend the first few days in Tennessee choking down great tablespoons of Milk of Magnesia, chickens nonplussed as I dashed, mewling like a fox kit, back and forth through the feed lot to the privy.

My mother—an innocent, bless her heart—had done nothing untoward to invite the man's advances. The driver lost interest somewhere south of Paint Lick. I had no way of knowing at the time, but I was writing my first short story, composing draft after draft in the dark as we rolled through Kentucky, gaining in elevation, revising for heightened pathos, and mounting panic. Jealousy was certainly a major theme. Nascent sexual desire, however misplaced, a powerful undercurrent. In the hands of a better writer, at least a more imaginative one, I might have muscled the suddenly stricken driver down into the exit well, commandeered the moving bus, radioed our position, and delivered all passengers to safety, executing a one-chance-in-hell belly landing, a bespectacled, pint-sized, crewcut Sully. But writing such a story would violate the unconscious pact I had with my father in which he, not I, played hero to my fretting nebbish, a mere boy, in thrall to him.

And so, we huddled, three of us in the back of the bus, swept along through the long, dark night, waiting for dawn's indifferent sentry to give our papers a cursory look before waving us through to morning in the New South.

Andrew Collard
AUTOTOPIA
Sterling Heights, MI

Stay hungry, the Liquor-Lotto sign says, long after
its abandonment, *stay hungry,* the cloud of mosquitos
responds behind its back
                         along the narrowing bank
of my very first river. I pull in off Van Dyke Ave toward
a rental counter vacant fifteen years, its storefront
holding space, now,
                 for only speculation. Autotopia,
the evidence of yesterday is unmistakable. What I remember
is as tenuous as what you have replaced it with: I have hit
the latest locally famous potholes,
                        I have ordered a Coke
alone at a bar named The Gathering Place, I have waved
to passersby come to worship among the lanes
of what was once a bowling alley
                          and will later return home
to my assigned drive in another city. It's easy to forget
the bluegrass, too, must migrate, that the hobby store is franchised
and headquartered in the south.
                   The plant full of robots
up the road constructing circuit boards for weapons didn't
come from nowhere, is not a foregone conclusion any more
than the 7-Eleven on the corner is:
                        there is nothing present here
that is not lost in its own transition, these once-bare lots
now flush with industry. Despite the testimony of the nails
pitched from the Video King's old marquee,
                             circled ominously
before the window, there was nothing wrong with following
my father through aisles of grainy VHS boxes, there was
nothing wrong with the inconvenience
                       of borrowing them
three-at-a-time, of waiting twenty minutes for a pizza
one door over, in a place we could afford to be —
to simplify any lineage,
             even this, is to betray it.

Ephraim Scott Sommers
ODE TO THIS, US ON A WINTER DAY, STARING OUT THE WINDOW AT THE NEW WORLD

imagine a bowling alley   empty
before the first ball
is ever let go of
in the morning
and a bartender
sorting one-dollar bills
for the bank
in her drawer
no house music
no crackle of busted speakers
and all the obedient pins
just standing there
in a pyramid
like soldiers
like so many of us
who are waiting
to be shouldered down
by the same hard blue throw
of another workday
curling down the lane
at all of us
Ann   I will never ask you
for much more
than this simple
quiet routine
of you beside me
in our leather chair
in our own house
every morning
before our separate day shifts
this stillness
in our bourbon room
under the flannel blanket

while outside
snow goes on
stopping time
piling its white hush
over everything
and the imagined bartender
has just received word
that snow has cancelled
the routine for today
and while she is staring
at her phone
the bowling pins
reanimate back into their own lives
and disappear
so our day too Ann
yours and mine has been whited out
so we unzip out of our uniforms
and out of any imagined metaphor
so we too don our slippers
and tumble back
into our bedroom
like dice
who have refused
the game of being pushed
around by anyone else's hands
this coming stretch
of hours and hours
and hours is finally ours

Monica Finger
BUG JAR

When it gets to be about eight-thirty, it's time to grab our bikes
and head down to the Bug Jar. Yours is black and rides low
and is missing both its rubber handlebar covers.
Mine is a sky blue and neon green Kawasaki that my mom won
in 2000 from a Walmart contest entry. You're faster

on a bike than I am and you don't like to brake, so you make
figure-eights, going forward and coming back so as not to leave
me behind. The cool night air on a Bug Jar Saturday is full
of possibilities. Most likely we've had a Genny or two already.
Most likely you have a Genny or two in your leather trench coat

pockets (Oz doesn't search anyone's pockets, just says heyyy
and it's ten bones). We climb the Ford Street bridge hill
and speed down Mount Hope Avenue, over the 490
on the pedestrian crossing and roll right onto Marshall Street.
Arriving is the best part 'cause friends are already there

smoking in little groups on the curb. You hand me a Seneca
100 after we lock our bikes to a pole. One of many little rituals
we perform as citizens of the Bug Jar. See—I belong here
and twice so, 'cause I won't just be a listener. My hands will bleed
pounding skins on the hot riser and my blazing fast feet

will kick over Genny lights that soak into the drum rug. So see —
I belong here. This place was yours first, but you were not selfish,
holding the flyer-pasted door open for me to go in as deep
as I liked. That's how it was with us. You uncorked the bottle,
but it was me who dove straight to the bottom. But tonight

it's still 2014 or '15 and we lean our elbows on the sticky
bar to demand the first of many shots, which we'll supplement
with trips to the car-bar between sets, til the throbbing 210 bpm
bass drum and the ear-searing growl of the 5150 run all together
in a milk-n-honey river of noise. Baby, this is the promised land

or if we're still in the desert, you're manna from heaven, free-falling
like you do into hungry hands of men. Here you're a god, and I worship
with the wide-eyed zealotry of a proselyte. You'll soon find out
I have a real problem sticking to gods. But tonight it's Saturday-
into-Sunday and we are up to our ears in beers,

floating on lapping waves of voices. Tonight I'll topple over
tasting asphalt on the hazy ride home. Failing again to keep up
with you. This is the part where you're supposed to come back
for me, but when I look up, you've already crested the hill
past Flint Street and Vacuum Oil, disappearing in a billow

of curly wheat-brown hair musk leather and smoke, and that
is why, when I got the call, I couldn't come to look
at your body. I wanted to you remember you like this– a blur
of black motion in the night, too free to be caught.
a tab left open at the Bug Jar, a debt I can't afford to pay.

Andrew Jeter
THE CONCEIT

I found it in a drawer
beneath the Yahtzee dice
and the extra power
cable for my old phone,

a sympathy card in
pale greens with a
stamp already attached
but no address, no
written note to say,

I'm sorry that it has
come to this, the
inevitable end, the
moment when you will
notice the sun is in
the south, winter's light
strained through leafless
branches and frozen air.

But I can't remember who
it is supposed to be for,
who I had in mind
when I picked the card,
applied the stamp,
considered the message.

Except now, of course,
it is you I am thinking of,
still standing, shadowless
in summer's hot blazing,
thinking that nothing much
will ever change.

Brian Builta
OCTOBER 10
Tuesday

At nine o'clock in the morning the signal comes – the miracle of mama's body is being turned to ash. She never liked being hot, hated sweating, and now her skin and muscle blister and pop. Students are coming and going on campus, learning and growing and dying themselves, some soon, some later. The day progresses. I have salmon for lunch, salmon on a bed of Mexican risotto, and there are capers involved, and some kind of cream sauce. There is traffic, and later bills arrive in the mailbox. That night, we tell stories of mama, stories about when she was alive and vital. A force. It takes three hours to reduce a body to ash.

> Fall breeze in the trees
> arrives with morning sunlight.
> Your ashes – boxed.

B. A. Van Sise
SAN JUAN

For years after the fact I'd insist
that my mother hadn't died, just
left: no Marlboro Reds, no x-rays,
no *here* and *here*, no spreading tumor
that stops her sleep and then her legs,
no breath-hunger: no, she'd stepped out
to Paradise: maybe there she had a
new family, maybe a son she liked better,
a car in that trim she'd always wanted:
bright red. Not dead, no, she'd left for a
place that played only her favorite movies,
where every night was surf and
turf. I would never begrudge her wanting
something different, though from time to
time I'd wished she'd been at a spelling
bee, a graduation, seen me bring home
a girl. Sometimes, when traveling,
I swear I'll still see her: new
husband, the other son, a couple
grandkids. For some reason
there's always balloons -bright
red- and she's always on her
way to dinner out. Last night
I dined with her daughter-in-
law, found no flaw in the lobster.
Took a long walk home in the
warm spring air on the cobble
road that hugs the harbor,
didn't mind one bit the
time I was wasting, or
the money I'd spent,
because this, right here? This
is where she went.

Karly Vance
TESSELLATION

The lake has given me
Ten stones to use
To build an altar to you.
I have taken my time.

I waited for a day when
The waves' coughs went quiet.
I could see straight through,
Choose rocks smooth as new fruit,

Rocks, tigered and rubied
Until I take them
Sleeping from their bed
To dry gray in the sun.

I scattered them through town:
A constellation, a monument
Of negative space. You might say
That's no altar at all. You're right.

The magic is this: you can touch
Any one stone with your eyes closed
And see, plain as a dream,
That in its past life

It was tigered and rubied,
It was tucked in bed, a tessellation
On clay that could cloud clear water
Or become any body.

Katherine Roth
THE FEATHER OF A GULL

It was an uncommon time —
you, just out of the hospital
me, fearful of your dying

We drove North over the Bridge
defiant with courage
mimicking freedom

to a log cabin on a bay
where land curved like arms to hold all that water
and us, so in need of the holding

Hunter Moon rose like a shaman
quiet after all the noise —
abundant in its roundness

Forests of yellow leaves
falling like confetti
as though life was a celebration

You coming back to me —
to sleep again, to lace our hands
to stroll the shoreline following shadows

I found the feather
left behind on cold sand —
there were so many

Kara Penn
MURDER OF CROWS

It was the oscillating absence of light
in the way sun ducks in and out
of cloud that drove us outside,

a surprising gathering of neighbors
watching crows, like garish black kites,
diving from roof ledges, ripping open

their voices like metal envelopes.
For what? we wondered. Then one dark
pool of feathers lifted wing tips,

mistaken as sinkhole in sidewalk.
It had become something to fall into
and be lost. It was for this

that hundreds came —
their preened bodies weighting
the mature and arcing maples,

their beaks like burnished knives,
voices unbearably sharp
as they became cloak, descending

upon that broken, mislaid thing.
Crows and the shadows of crows.
Dark into dark.

Elizabeth Kerlikowske
DEMENTIA AND THE WILD MAN

Displacement
The giraffe is the Wild Man's memory. When he is distraught, she recounts his life: how he was a musician, then suddenly a soldier, then a woodworker. She reminds him of the loves of his life, leaving herself out because it's already too complicated. When he begins to add details or correct her, she knows he's back. The giraffe has memorized all the Wild Man's numbers, sorts his pills, knows the day his garbage will be picked up. Somedays, she feels like an elephant—even after he is gone, she will never forget.

The first step in lucid dreaming is to realize one is dreaming
When the Wild Man doesn't answer her knock, the giraffe looks out back. It's still early for him, but she sees movement on the ivy-covered hillside. He stoops, gathering invasive blossoms from garlic mustard, Japanese knotweed, and myrtle: all the blooms available this spring morning. *Stop*, he yells as he wanders toward the giraffe. *You almost stepped on Mom's grave!* At his feet the bleached skeleton of a deer, pulled apart by animals and the weather. The Wild Man drops the flowers between her long white bones. Ignoring the giraffe, he shuffles back to the house. A minute later, he is asleep in the living room: Bonanza, then Paladin.

Gentle Giant
Visitors are always surprised by the Wild Man's size, not just his wilderness. He used to call himself the gentle giant but his sense of himself in the world has shrunk. He still looks powerful, like an abandoned marble mansion, parts of it uninhabitable. His mouth, decayed. His hair, a gray ropy pack rat's nest. The hygiene of a hermit, which he has become, shoes taped together though the giraffe has gotten him several pairs and boots. Even now, even now, when the giraffe stands too close, she feels pulled toward the Wild Man's side and steps away. The panda observed that the last time they delivered groceries together, though he was smart enough not to say anything.

The difference between a collector and a hoarder is shelves
said the Wild Man before his shelves collapsed into heaps of Central American masks, silver and turquoise jewelry, and paperbacks. Deer shaman, a peyote lizard, and a corn protector mingle with Ixchel and Chac, gods of medicine,

rain and thunder in a heap. Mice peek out of their eye holes. The caretakers have determined this midden is worthless, what the Wild Man spent his life amassing. The face the giraffe wears when she visits him is not beaded, intricate, or colorful, but calm in its dappled years. The Wild Man balances on a rim of rage and acceptance but his face is a field half-cultivated, waiting for healing rain that will never come.

MIA
The Wild Man's door is open when the Giraffe arrives. She has been calling his phone for hours. Old 7/11 cups on his table no doubt gave him the idea to walk there. She's sure of it. Only bologna in his fridge. Fried chicken bones on the counter. Just four blocks each way and across a street. *Yeh, he come here*, says the tiger. *He want fry chicken; we don't have. He buy car air freshener. His wallet fall apart when he try to pay. Everything shove in pockets. Poor guy.* Back at the zoo, the giraffe hears shuffling behind her. A boy leads the Wild Man out of the woods, slowly. Twilight. The three of them can barely see each other. Thank you, says the Wild Man to the boy and presses the air freshener into his hand.

Months Become Years
The Wild Man likes the dog, Naomi. With a dog, you don't have to guess their feelings. The zookeepers bring her. Often she gets close enough to pet. She is excited by the variety of crumbs caked on the floor. The Wild Man doesn't remember a specific zookeeper. They are all shaped like piles of mashed potatoes. They bring his food. The camel stops by Saturdays with food. The giraffe rolls his dumpster to the curb Mondays. "I am a big baby who everyone takes care of," he says, as if it should be this way. Every three weeks, he changes his clothes, never his idea.

Forlorn
The giraffe feels estranged from the Wild Man. He is getting worse. He forgets he can call for help, for food. Sometimes he stares into the past midbite and holds his sandwich in front of him as if he's reading it. The garbage he relies on other people to throw away he at least stacks neatly on the filthy counters. He is comfortable with only dirty silverware and unrinsed Meals on Wheels trays divided up like elementary school lunch, and the carcass of the fried chicken the camel brings on Saturdays. The camel too is tired of the losing battle. *Do the math*, he says. *Three zookeepers, a giraffe and a camel=one Wild Man. It's neither efficient nor cost-effective.*

No Forwarding Address
The giraffe was away for a month. The camel texted about his unhappiness with the zookeepers. The zookeepers texted about how they were hiring another zookeeper to take care of the Wild Man. That made six and the little dog, Naomi. The giraffe pulls in the Wild Man's driveway. A window ledge has rotted off the house. No one has mowed and it's June. More limbs have fallen on the garage. The house is "open to casual entry" as police say. No power. The giraffe can't tell if it's been ransacked because it looks like it did when the Wild Man lived here. She is out of the loop. No. She has escaped the loop. She calls the post office. She makes her way to the basement and takes all the silver rings inlaid with turquoise. Not because she wants them, but because they were valuable to him.

Hutches
the Wild Man built for other wild things dot the woods behind the private zoo. Twigs and berry canes and bark, igloos of the Midwest. Each marked with a thin oily rag impaled on a dowel and somewhere a GI Joe. The Wild Man doesn't go outside in winter, but the giraffe wanders back there on her visits. She blends in with the oaks who keep their leaves till spring. The boy with an old Polaroid has set numbered cards in front of some hutches. He presses the arrow, hears the whirr. The picture spits out. He is surprised by the giraffe in the background but not scared. He takes a selfie, looks at it and sees his condor. He doesn't tell anyone.

Meghan Sterling
WINTER IS AN UNRELIABLE NARRATOR

Where I come from, in February, lemons are
heavy on the trees. I used to smell them on
my hands, on the inside of my wrists. Lemon
perfume. Lemon syrup. A mountain of lemons
to climb and proclaim myself queen of lemons.
I pretend I wake up in a lemon grove, that I have
a table ankle deep in grass, hidden under the waxy
leaves where I serve meals to my friends. Beneath
the yellow fruit, all of our smiling yellow faces.
Our reality is winter's cold palm slapping our cheeks
bloodless, the ground steel. My husband thinks we
should play the Civil War documentary soundtrack
most mornings. Mournful violins, a reminder of struggle.
I wonder how we ended up here, then I remember. I want
to do it all again and I am not sure I could survive it.

Kenton K. Yee
MOON PIE LOVER

Because your silent beauty shines through
only on clear nights, clouds induce anxiety
in me. Every night is unpredictable and
I stress your shine's return as I do lightning,
bills, and the mosquito population, my dear
luminous coin, spherical angel, baby face,
canine temptress, pale blue high beam, spy
balloon, volleyball, snowdrop, second sun,

meaning I dig you more than all planets
and stars—the whole clockwork—combined,
meaning I want you to come for me tonight.
We'll swim with koi in Golden Gate Park.
I'll nibble the soft marshmallow between
your crackers until you're full and bright.

Anita Hunt
CANNING SUNLIGHT

We pick the ripening rays,
place them in the basin of our heart.
Some days are swallowed whole,
others sliced and seasoned,
sealed in jars to keep us through the dark.
A torn and folded recipe passed in sleep,
tucked between cushions and under the sink.
Kept in shadowed pantries
to hold the flavor of a golden day.

Most of us have been measuring wrong;
it's best to add more than you think you'll need.
So much evaporates over the years.
Sweetness hides in bitter branches
until the fruit has pushed through
and fallen, bruised, bright as May.

Ellen Stone
QUART MASON JARS

He collects them. Cleans them up.
Stores jars on the many shelves
of the dirt cellar, his cluttered mind.

Containers, spaces to put
things: worries, beans, bills.
His own tomato sauce that takes days —

when the house smelled like basil
perfuming the old lath, seeping
into walls like too much weeping.

Dad remembers what pluck
sounds like – gripped sleek, peeled
& chunked, tucked snug like so

many children, scattered now.
I probably thought he blew alum
from tops of clouds, sour from rain

fronts lasting days. Another hemlock
morning, blue curve of horizon
ribboning rivers behind glass.

We counted luck in quart jars
when we were kids. A good day
was seven, at least. Enough to fill

the canner, bring it to a hard boil.

April Yu
SOLSTICE

Thanksgiving came and went. There was no turkey that year, no stuffing or cider or those croutons from TV with garlic seeds that snapped white-hot between your teeth. We didn't sit at home like a nice family.

"Where's Daddy?" Henry asked me as the leaves fell crisp and crimson into the lawn.

"He's away," I said.

"He's not coming back, is he?" Amelie asked. She had a way of saying things that grated on me, like every word was a fact.

"He'll come back." When I was younger and alone, I drew pictures on the mantle for each hour he was gone and covered every inch of plaster in blazing neon marker. He wasn't happy when he returned, wasn't happy at all. But I didn't mind it because he was there.

The next day I refused pumpkin pie at the school cafeteria. No one swept the leaves off the lawn.

My father celebrated Thanksgiving once. He had Mommy clean dead rabbits, and I brought out a tablecloth and we feasted like princes. Then the next year all he had strength for was bottles and bottles of clear liquid that he told me was water but didn't really smell like it, and the dead rabbits faded into the edges of Mommy's eyes, and then she was on the driveway telling me she was leaving.

"Mommy," I said. For some reason the bottles at home scared me, and when I closed my eyes, I didn't see the lambs Mommy taught me about, just Daddy with his eyes scratched out into oozing translucent gashes. "Mommy, please."

She was packing all her stuff into the car. Lipstick and teabags and things. "You can't come with me."

"I'll help you." She knew I was a helper; I helped all the time. With Daddy when he fell asleep, with the envelopes that flooded our mailbox. I was a good helper.

"No, you won't." She wouldn't even look at me. "Stay here. Help your father. He needs it."

"He hates it when I help him."

She slammed the trunk closed and slid into the front door seat.

"Please, Mommy." I was screaming then like some common animal, limbs thrashing, banging on the door. "Let me in!"

She closed her eyes. "I can't do this anymore."

"I'll help you. I'll help you."

"He'll kill me."

"I need you! Don't leave me!"

"Bye, baby," she whispered, stepping on the gas.

"MOMMY!"

I watched her disappear into the woods, leaves falling everywhere, car fading into nothing as I wailed and wailed until I thought I might break in two on the empty driveway. Daddy watched me from the porch with his oozing translucent eyes.

Our father could be a kind man. Two years ago, he played with Henry in the backyard like he was a firstborn, making snow angels, hunting squirrels. Amelie gave him her doll and he wrote ANDY in huge block letters on her boot like the movie character. My stepmother massaged his neck whenever he had trouble moving around. I watched it all through my bedroom window. They looked like a nice family.

Two years later, I watched the leaves fall through the window. They didn't make a sound.

"You were just lying to Henry, right?" Amelie asked.

"Don't come into my room."

"I know you were lying."

"You'll get yourself hurt," I said, because she was standing in the doorway looking thin and papery, as if one slight wind might blow her away.

"I'm brave. I can handle it."

"I wasn't lying." The hole between her teeth gaped as she spoke. "He always comes back. He wouldn't just leave."

"But Mom already…"

"Get out!" I slammed the door.

Ten years ago, when my stepmother first brought Amelie back from the hospital, frost glittered on the pavement. Amelie was a crying mass of fat, arms bunched, straining toward the silver sky.

"I don't know what to do," I said.

"Just hold her."

"That's okay." I might drop her.

My stepmother sighed, irritation dripping in her throat. "Don't you care about us at all?"

"What?"

"This family. We try our hardest for you. You could at least pretend to be happy."

Words clogged in my throat. I held the fucking baby.

Days passed. Our lawn overflowed, crimson and gold and brown. I couldn't ask the twins to rake without them asking questions and I couldn't go outside without smelling blood.

Henry made the lunch sandwiches and Amelie signed the parent slips and I bought groceries with money I couldn't repay.

"Do you think Daddy's going to find Mommy?" Henry asked, eyes like shallow basins.

"Maybe."

"Mommy said she wasn't coming back." Amelie looked down.

"Even if Daddy begged."

"He would never beg." Not anyone. Not for anything.

When my stepmother left, the frozen air cracked open with her blood. My dad smashed her head into the closet. Or the cupboard. Or the mantle, smeared with my old drawings: neon cats, dogs, stick people in the park.

I don't really remember because when I cleaned everything up after, I didn't hear Henry's cries, the explosion of the engine. I just scrubbed every surface of our three-room house with the orange walls and faded brown carpets until it smelled like vinegar and bleach. I used both, always, just in case one didn't work.

Dying things always came in bright colors. He didn't come back.

When I turned ten, I followed my father into the woods hoping he would teach me to hunt. It was the only birthday gift I'd ever asked of him: to shoot a squirrel straight through the eye with its fur, blood, guts intact. The rifle looked new when it wasn't against Mommy's head. He fitted my hand at the trigger. We waited in the cold spring frost. I could sense his stubbly chin, the sharp scent of aftershave, a peripheral of the sheen in his oily eyes. I trembled.

He slapped my hand. "Focus."

When the gunshot sounded, when the squirrel fell, I thought he might love me.

The bread and cheese ran out. There were no more field trips. The bank caught up to us before I knew to run.

"We need Daddy." Henry was crying again and I almost hated him for it. "Please call him."

"I can't."

"Why?"

"It's too expensive."

"It's okay. Just this once. We need it," Amelie said.

I wanted to tell her to shut up. She had no idea what she was talking about.

"Don't tell me what to do."

Henry began to wail, the sobs bursting out of his chest like a sputtering car engine. It cut me deeper than the winter wind.

"Go outside."

Amelie stared at the floor, then dragged Henry outside. The front door slammed shut.

For the seventieth time, I fell to the floor and called our father, and for the seventieth time, I listened to it go to voicemail. I heard my voice break out of myself: *Come back. We need you. Please, Daddy. Come back.*

Every morning we went out to shoot, his hands over mine, squirrels evolved to rabbits evolved to beavers. When the sun got hot, we cleaned the kills into glistening spoils. If I closed my eyes, every time he guided my arms to the target could have been an embrace.

When he finally stopped teaching me, I found him kissing a young woman at our doorstep. I watched him look almost happy as he forgot my mother. I watched how they shared a glass of wine and laughed like it had all been a cruel joke.

I ran. I ran until the sweat and wind drowned me. For a second the gun held itself in my hands. I threw it in the trees, gasped for air, and never went into the woods again.

Winter wind howled in through the trees, clawing the skin off my back until I was bloodless, gutless.

"Maybe he's—"

"Shut up, Henry." Amelie's eyes glistened. "I told you. He isn't coming back. They were both lying. He isn't coming back!"

I watched my hand slap across her face, scarlet blooming like a wildflower. The sound came after. Glasses shattering.

"Don't you blame this on me." I was trembling. *Focus*. "This isn't my fault!"

Amelie's eyes were wide, iridescent. "Then tell me the truth."

"Don't be so calm. Don't act so righteous!"

She didn't say anything, just breathed.

"He's going to come back whether he likes it or not!"

Her cheek patterned purple.

Henry ran for my leg and began to cry.

The frost crept in through the window and up my bones until I couldn't get up for days. Henry's tears froze. We wouldn't survive until Christmas dinner.

"What are you doing?"

"Get out of my room."

"You're leaving," Amelie said.

"I'm trying to live."

"You're just going to leave us here?" She stood in the doorway, watching clothes bundle into my arms, her body a glass pane painted crimson. One touch and it might shatter. "You're going to make me take care of Henry alone?"

"Don't be selfish."

If I could just get to the kitchen. If I could just get something to eat. I could disappear.

"I don't know what to do. I don't know how."

I could disappear from this house that was more dead than alive. I could disappear and not smell blood on my hands every time I closed my eyes. I could disappear without a shadow to remember me by.

"You'll learn." Downstairs. Bread tucked into my pockets. "You'll have to."

"Please."

I opened the door. Henry still slept in his room of ghosts. "He never wanted me anyway."

"Please!" Glasses shattering. "I need you! Don't leave me!"

The winter wind clawed my body away.

The ghosts still knew how to rise in my sleep. Little girls screaming. Little boys mauled in their sleep. A gun telling me it loved me. A car breaking my body open. The woods caged me into myself.

I need you. Don't leave me. I had become my father. *I don't know what to do. I don't know how.*

Was he brave for leaving us? Was he brave for not coming back? Could he have searched through the three pairs of shallow basin eyes and found what he had chased all his life?

I tasted the steel and smoke before I found it, picked it out of the spiraling snow. The gun held my hand like a childhood. By then I was so hungry my stomach could have clawed out of my body.

I could end this. I could tell myself it had been brave.

When I turned back toward the house, I could have called it hunger or delirium or my body collapsing, but all I could think about was how my mother's car had ribboned into the dark, how my father had cut himself away like a puppet on a string, how Henry clung to hope like a home. How Amelie fractured herself with reality and still believed in something more.

The gun trembled in my hands. *Bang.* The gunshot sounded, a beaver fell, and the ghosts fell away like applause. I was going to survive.

I cleaned the kill and devoured it like a king. When dawn rose soft over the tree line, I closed my eyes and made a snow angel. It could have been Christmas Day.

Jason Gordy Walker
FATHER TO SON

The creases on your cheek resembled mine
but nothing else took on my shape besides
your hands beneath the moon's full light that turned
the corner like the stranger walking slowly
toward the neighbor's car that idled soft
as leaves upon the tilting grass. The door
was shut, and he was off with someone's wife,
exhaust a whisper in the night, and then
I saw your eyes as dark as crows. They flew
into my deepest fear, astounding what
they found in there. My mouth lit up with words
I knew you'd never hear, although I'd watched
you all these years: the steps you took without
me there, the times you fell, or pulled your hair,
the car you drove for miles alone, the jokes
you made to Mom at home, the food you ate,
the clothes you wore, the books you read, the notes
you tore, the dogs and cats you raised yourself,
the films you watched, the things you felt, and all
the time I had no choice because I lost
my mind and voice to this great void you feel
but never see. I'm here but not, I'm gone
yet found. If night can fall without a sound,
then scratch my name into the ground, or wait,
just wait and think a while until you hear
me say, "My son, I wish to see your face
in sun for once." And, no, I know your ears,
now old and deaf, can't hear my silent breath,
yet picture your father if you can, stick-
like figure in the sand, a moonstruck man.

Roger D'Agostin
PLUMBING

I was going through photos trying to decide. You want a nice mix. Young, old, and of course, people that will be at the wake. Not too many predeceased. That's why I only included one with her two sisters. They're sitting at my mom's dining room table and I think it's Christmas because they're all wearing turtlenecks and I know people don't break out turtlenecks just for Christmas, but still, I'm pretty sure.

I could ask my mom. She's not dead. She's actually healthy. She lives independently, still drives (only in the morning), and volunteers at her church (but she does get picked up). But this year I've already taken her to six wakes and she's very critical. Her cousin Chester didn't have a photo of his parents. I reminded her Chester fathered eighteen children with three wives and a girlfriend. He had twenty-three grandchildren. "It's his mother and father for Christ's sake," Mom snapped. That's when I decided I needed to prepare.

In most of the ones I've decided on, she's smiling, but around seventy, it stopped. It's not even a close-mouthed grin. Rather I'm-here-get-the-picture-over-with-already-for-Christ's-Sake. So every family picture for the last seventeen years sucks. I stopped posting them on Facebook when friends privately messaged me to ask if she's OK. I don't want someone asking me at her wake.

In my mom's house, there are twelve steps from the garage to the first floor. Mom navigates them like a chimp, bent over, one hand on two steps in front of her, the other holding her cane, lifting her left foot, then the right, counting each one. My sister thinks the exercise outweighs the risks. I think the opposite. That's why I bring up an alternative.

"Mom, they have these electric chairs that attach to the bannister and it brings you up the stairs like an elevator. Maybe we can look into having one installed."

The first time I mention this, she says she'll think about it, but a week later it turns to no.

She did this with the dining room table too. Mom has this horrible dining room set from the seventies but set's not the right word. It's an oval Formica table attached to a booth that surrounds the table. There's one entry. Not an opening where you can go right or left. Only left. Growing up our order was me, my brother Greg, then my sister Mary, Dad, then Mom at the end. No exceptions. Even if Mary was sitting in the booth doing homework when dinner time came around, she wouldn't just slide in. She got up to let me enter then waited for Greg. The only position that made sense was Mom's because she was constantly going back and forth to the kitchen. Everyone else, except Dad to some extent, was trapped, unable to leave until the person before them did.

Family gatherings were pure terror. We had an order for those too and my place was between Aunt Lorraine and Aunt Macy. We were the last three and when dinner ended, at least when I had finished my dinner, they never left. They'd sit and talk and nudge me with questions about school or baseball or whatever holiday they were here for, and I was forbidden to ask them to slide out. I waited until one of them had to use the bathroom. When I got older, I tried to force as much beverage into them as possible.

We passed this trauma on to my nieces and nephews. They got big on whispering *don't get trapped* every time we all got together which we always did at Mom's because Mary lived two hours south in Jersey and Greg just over the border in Rhode Island. I had drawn the unmarried straw and remained local in Connecticut.

But last Christmas we went to Greg's and for Easter, Mary's, because the previous Easter Mom had snapped at Greg's daughter, "No one's trapped." She was also having problems with the kitchen sink and the toilet. She said she met a retired plumber who still did odd jobs. He used to have a decent-sized plumbing business with a few vans—QC Plumbing—but when Covid hit he had to let everyone go and he decided to retire. She didn't give me his name.

Not even when I asked again after he installed a toilet seat with a higher profile on the main floor (which made sense) and redid the bathtub so it was now a shower with a seat, non-slip floor, and handholds (which also made sense). She told me she was having the same changes made to the bathroom on the second floor which made no sense because she never goes up to the second floor.

This is when I brought up the kitchen "set." I watched her slides in and out become increasingly unsteady, with her cane, having to step backwards, and I thought it would be best to make a change to this furniture first, and then perhaps the second-floor bathroom.

I thought we left it as a topic we still needed to discuss but the next time I stopped over, the old toilet was in the garage.

"I don't want you calling the plumber anymore, Mom."
"I will most certainly call the plumber if I need to."
"Well, I want to know."
"You don't need to know."

So, I called the plumber, Jack O'Neill (it wasn't difficult with Google since I knew the name of his business) and lied. "Look, my mom is really sensitive about this but she's been diagnosed with dementia. It's in its early stages so you're probably not going to notice, but anyhow I'm her Power of Attorney so when she calls, could you let me know? Just so I can make sure you get paid."

He said, "Of course, no problem, Mr. Andersen."
"Don't tell her."
"No. I won't. I mean nothing's going to change."
"Good. Just don't tell her."

Two weeks later he called.
"The shower head is dripping."
"She probably doesn't turn the knob hard enough." Jack didn't say anything. "Tell her you have time next week and I'll get over there this weekend and take a look."
"Can you get over there tonight?"
"Not tonight."
"She told me you live in Norwalk."
"I do but I can't get over there tonight."
"Tomorrow?"
"Jack, this weekend is fine."
"I just thought you might be able to get over there sooner."
"Let's wait, Jack."
"Look they don't make hardware like they used to. I know. I'm seventy-four and I sound old saying this, but it's true. Everything's chrome plated. And there's no quality control. The thickness, not to mention grade of brass isn't consistent. I see this all the time. If it's just a matter of her not turning it all the way I won't charge her. She knows that. Look, I'm going to stop by tomorrow anyway. I'll take a look."

The van's in the driveway when I arrive, the removed QC Plumbing lettering legible, a lighter shade of dirty white. The garage door is open and I head up to the main floor. Mom's sitting in the dining room booth with Jack. She is not on the end. I can see, even though their backs are to me, that they're looking down at the table. She's saying, "Yes, yes." They're both holding the shower head. He's pointing at her end. Mom's nodding and smiling. Then she sees me. Her mouth suddenly flatlines, as if I were about to take a family picture.

LeAnn Peterson
LOVE AND KNITTING

"Knock, knock," I say and tap on the door to her room in the memory care unit. She's sitting in her recliner, but I can't tell if she is asleep or not. The bright early afternoon sun is streaming through the windows, and I can only see her in shadow. I can tell the cleaning staff has been in her room. The air is saturated with an almost nauseating aroma from a syrupy sweet floral antiseptic spray. My eyes adjust to the light in her room. I glance around for a quick inspection. The bed is made and everything looks tidy.

She turns her head toward me and eyes the shopping bag over my arm. She asks, "Did you bring me a present?"

"Kind of," I say as I walk to her closet. There are clean clothes on the hangers. I pull out a folding chair propped against the closet's inside wall and set the chair so I am facing her. Taking out a skein of yarn and a pair of knitting needles from the bag, I hold them up. "Remember?" I ask. "Remember the last time I was here? You asked me to bring knitting stuff the next time I visited you."

"I was hoping maybe you brought me some ice cream." She smiles as I give her the needles and yarn. Watching her smooth the variegated acrylic fiber with the palm of her hand and then roll the tip of the metal knitting needle between her right thumb and forefinger brings back a childhood memory.

I am six, recovering from strep throat, and bored. She digs through her craft box and finds one skein of sky-blue yarn and a pair of silver aluminum needles. For the next five days after lunch, we sit on the sofa, and she teaches me how to cast on and work a garter stitch. I want to get my piece of knitting long enough for a scarf. She examines each finished row to make sure I haven't dropped, added, or twisted any stitches.

Now, our roles are reversed. I watch her fingers awkwardly manipulate the yarn trying to cast on stitches for a foundation row. "Like this?" "Like that?" she asks and holds her work out at arm's length for my approval. Her knitting gauge is too tight, which makes it almost impossible to push the working needle into a completed stitch and rotate it to create a new one. She is baffled by any help I try to give her. Like her brain, the yarn is full of tangles and knots.

She stops trying to knit and rubs the soreness in her wrists. "I'm going to ask you a question," she says and spends a few seconds studying my face. Then, as if we were acquaintances having a casual conversation over a cup of tea, she wants to know, "Who is your mother?"

My heart sinks. Today is the first time she has forgotten I am her daughter. This memory lapse startles and scares me. How can she not know me?

She waits patiently for my answer. I take a deep breath and say, "Well, Mom, you are—you are my mom!"

"Oh!" she gasps with astonishment. "I'm so glad! I am just so glad because I just love you!" Relief flickers over her face. At this moment, she knows who I am, she knows that she loves me, and it is enough.

She picks up the needles and yarn. This time, I stand behind her chair and drape my arms over her shoulders. "I love you, too, Mom," I say and cover her hands with mine. Together, we place yarn between the working needles and manage to make a new stitch while anticipating the ones to follow. The needles click against each other. Love and knitting are all that matter for now.

Robert Fanning
JARÐHITI // GEOTHERMAL

It's good to be thin-skinned and naïve, new to any land. The older you get, the more you know, the less you are. Buried in icesheets of knowledge and sleep. Forgetting the fires that woke you. Flushed cheeks, that blush you'd feel at another touch. Remember? Here, come in from the cold. Let me take you inside, bake you some bread. Let me remind you with sweat, with sway of steam. My heat, your heat— in this sacred pool. Desire is what every body is made of. Underneath. Once and always. The eternal breath. This deep and holy hearth.

Mary Dean Lee
TASTE OF YOU

She reaches for the white peach
biting down, skin still on,
juice splashing, tart and sweet.
He peels his and cuts it in
pieces, fingers opening her
mouth to place a chunk
on her tongue, his lips finding
splatters on chin and breast.
Her strings vibrate taut, high,
she stumbles in a panic out to the
sea past the breakers to calm water
where she floats on her back
letting the undertow pull her
slow, soft down the shore.
Tomorrow she will explore
his finger in her mouth,
test her teeth against his nail.

Monica Rico
ROUNDING CAPE HORN

It's funny   I don't remember   when I stopped
closing   my eyes   when you   kissed me
I liked   watching   your eyes   close   I liked seeing   you
trust me   trust   I would not   move   and offer
    my mouth to yours
    every
    time   it's funny   I don't
    remember   when   you stopped
closing   yours   maybe I   quickly closed
    mine   and you   liked watching   me mo
    toward you   and you liked   seeing me   trust you
trust I would   hold still   and kiss you   funny   I do
    remember   the exact reason   when we kissed
    and stopped   closing our eyes   I liked looking
into yours   I liked when your eyes   became b
    a bright blue   only the sky   can do   over
    a body of water   I drink
    then ask you   to drink   I like watching you
    dissolve
    into the sky
    you like seeing   me green   wings open   op
open

B. A. Van Sise
LABOR DAY, BROOKLYN

The Romans, to greet, would lean in and kiss
each other's eyes. Sometimes I wish to be
that delicate and that dangerous, to have my

lips be the only thing you see. To be in
the world and still want the world. It is,
this morning, raining. Burn a candle, cancel

a plan. Run your hands through your hair
and hear that, far off, outside even today
there is a parade: a long line of

bodies marching in rough lines, lining
the streets of Brooklyn with all the
sounds we cannot see, their drums

banging out Valentine rhythms. Sometimes
I regret the fall of Rome, wish to comb
your curls with my fingers, wish to cross

that dark river after pressing
your breasts to my eyes, two
soft coins to fund the ferryman.

He'd lean in, thank me, kiss
my lashes, tell me this is
the finest fee yet, and set

to the far shore to forget my name.
And so the water falls
from the sky, drapes

the roofs as your shirt
does the floor, all the
while with a thousand men,

a thousand drums nearing.
And you made me want to be
what I was always meant to be:

a hundred thousand raindrops
seeding the sky, and
                                              then disappearing.

B. A. Van Sise
ARTIFACT

>*Artifact, n. from the Latin* arte, *'using art'*
>*and* factum, *'something made'*

For years we had tried to rid
ourselves of the awkward ways we'd bid
adieu — touch a hand and not a glove,
say we'd love to make plans for

some other time, as if some other
time is a thing that could ever exist,
as if we'd not missed a chance
to put a change to all of this.

Who knew our cheeks could be so wide
that kissing them our lips would almost touch?
And, though, the thought we thought we hid:
oh, oh how, we wish they did.

John Flesher
KNOW WHEN TO RUN

They had me. Had me, dead to rights. I knew it an instant after our cars zipped past each other on lonely, two-lane highway 77 in Michigan's Upper Peninsula back in the spring of 2010. Glancing in the rear-view mirror, I saw their brake lights illuminate the darkness and winced as they made a sweeping U-turn, zoomed back my way, and activated red and blue flashers. Dammit. My speedometer read sixty-two. On a busier road, they'd probably have ignored me. Who heeds the fifty-five-mile-per-hour limit, anyway? But this was the sparsely populated U.P., and my vehicle might well have been the only one they'd seen for miles. Busted.

I'd gotten a few speeding tickets over the years and knew the drill. Stopping along the bumpy roadside, I rolled down the window with license, registration, and insurance cards ready for inspection. "Do you know why I stopped you tonight, sir?" They always ask that. How to respond? Play dumb and say I have no idea, or acknowledge my transgression and throw myself on the mercy of the cop? I've tried both, usually for naught. On this occasion, ducking away from the piercing glare of the state police officer's flashlight, I stammered something like, "I'm not quite sure." Not very convincing. The trooper said the radar had clocked me at sixty-six, which seemed excessive but hardly worth debating.

That's when things went from been there, done that to bizarre.

I expected the officer to return to his cruiser and write up a citation. Instead, he looked fixedly at me and asked, "Why are you acting so nervous, sir?"

I responded with a shaky chuckle that I didn't realize I was giving that impression. Then came a curve-ball question that had never been thrown my way before: "Are you carrying anything illegal? Any contraband?"

"*Contraband?* No," I responded incredulously. Before I could ask where on earth he got that idea, something—the rustle of footsteps, perhaps, or the flicker of a second light beam in the corner of my eye—alerted me to the presence of another trooper on the passenger's side. Both in their late twenties to early thirties, I guessed; medium height, husky, and wearing standard uniforms with dark blue shirts, blue-gray pants, neckties, and hats. Could they be pegging me as a crook? A dope smuggler? Maybe the car I was driving fit the profile. Maybe I did, too?

Completely untrue, of course; easy to debunk. Nevertheless, an uneasy feeling crept over me. A sense that I must have done something wrong, something more than just being a tad lead-footed, something that could land me in deep trouble. It wasn't logical, but that hardly seemed to matter.

A wire service correspondent in those days, my mission was writing stories of nationwide interest about Michigan's northlands. Arriving from my native South in the winter of 1992, I was captivated by the landscape's stark, icy hardness. I seized any opportunity to visit the deep woods, which brought occasional encounters with deer or moose and a profound quietness, interrupted only by the rustle of windblown treetops, birds' chirps and gurgling of pebbly streams.

I covered battles over logging, mining, and other economic development projects in wild places, each a clash of values and visions for living off the land—and with it. One in particular drew my attention, as the Kennecott company sought to drill a nickel mine in the Upper Peninsula's Yellow Dog Plains, beneath a Lake Superior tributary and a sixty-foot-high outcrop sacred to the Keweenaw Bay Indian Community. Government agencies approved permits after a decade of wrangling.

With groundbreaking imminent in spring of 2010, a small group of activists occupied the grounds and refused to leave. A source tipped me late one afternoon that police and security guards were planning a raid. The disputed area was a five-hour drive from my home. I had to get up there. Pronto.

Problem was, my family had just one car and my wife needed it, so I booked a rental. To my delight, a clerk at the Enterprise counter informed me the only thing available on such short notice was a swanky, sky-blue convertible. I'd never driven one. How cool it would be to cruise with the top down across the five-mile-long Mackinac Bridge, which towers above the swirling straits connecting lakes Michigan and Huron! Florida license plates, I noted, while stowing my gear in the trunk. Maybe it had been driven here by one of those "snowbird" retirees coming north for the summer.

Later that night, those tags would have more sinister implications for a couple of state police troopers who pulled me over, apparently convinced they'd nabbed a breaking-bad guy. "I'm a reporter with The Associated Press," I tried to explain as the officer grilled me about supposed "contraband." I offered my media credential, which usually was accorded at least a bit of respect. The trooper brushed it away with a smirk. Maybe he thought it was a fake. He conferred with his partner, then asked more questions about what I was carrying. Tired and growing impatient, I made an offer that I figured would resolve matters quickly, although it probably would have horrified a defense attorney: Did they want to search the car?

The lawman's eyes widened in eager surprise. "Could we?"

"Certainly," I replied, opening the door and climbing out. "You're not going to find anything except my stuff but look all you want."

I hoped they would reward my helpfulness by cutting me a break on the speeding. But I froze as the guy ran a hand up and down my legs. I, a law-abiding citizen with a squeaky-clean record, was being *frisked*—for the first time ever! Not one of those hard-core, hands-against-the-wall, feet-back-and-spread-'em frisks like I'd seen on TV, but nonetheless I was being physically checked for a weapon. It felt eerie. Offensive, even.

I stepped toward the second officer, who had opened the car's trunk and was rummaging through my duffel bag. "Stay right here," the first one said, grasping my right arm.

It dawned on me that I'd made a big mistake. A cop who suspected me of wrongdoing was searching my vehicle and I couldn't watch! What if the previous renter had stashed drugs somewhere inside? Or what if, in their zeal to nab someone they *knew* was a smuggler, the officers planted false evidence to frame me? Okay, that was probably silly, the stuff of movie thrillers, but...*what if?* At one point, the second trooper rushed over with a plastic bag of pills. "What's this?" he demanded.

"It's *Claritin!*" I said pleadingly. "Antihistamine. I have allergies." Trooper Number One waved off the find but instructed his partner to keep looking.

I stood there by the side of the road, feeling the gentle breeze, the hardness of the pavement beneath my feet, the embarrassment of being in this position. Trooper Number Two moved to the back seat, then the front, training his beam across and beneath the seats. The squad car's lights kept flashing, mosquitoes swarmed, and suddenly I was gripped by a rising sense of panic, a nearly irresistible urge to run somewhere, anywhere. My breaths became shallow and rapid. My heart was racing; it seemed as if a drum was pounding in my ears.

My eyes darted about. Little was visible, but I knew there were thick woods on both sides of the road. Maybe I could give these guys the slip, then call an editor to vouch for me or get a lawyer. A crazy notion, but one side of my brain was screaming at me to act on it—*GET OUT OF HERE! NOW!*—while the other side was yelling just as loudly: *STAY PUT, YOU FOOL!* My muscles twitched. I was poised to take flight, so close…but my feet seemed rooted to the spot, as though paralyzed. I don't know what I'd have done if the search had lasted much longer, but blessedly, Trooper Number Two—having concluded his chore by getting on hands and knees to examine my car's underside—walked up and shook his head. I took a deep breath and felt the tension ease.

Trooper Number One offered what seemed a halfhearted apology, explaining that my demeanor and the Florida-registered convertible had been red flags. No hard feelings, I replied, and slipped behind the wheel again, my t-shirt damp with sweat. They still didn't appear entirely convinced of my innocence, but neither objected as I took off, my speeding transgression apparently forgotten. They followed a while as I dawdled along, well below the limit, before finally zooming past me and fading into the blackness.

I drove another forty minutes or so before stopping for the night at a Comfort Inn on the outskirts of Munising. A nearby unincorporated village called Christmas has a tribal casino with a log cabin-like exterior and an angular green roof. I sipped a whiskey sour at the bar, then wandered over to the Lake Superior waterfront, shivering in the chilly darkness, listening to waves lapping against a seawall.

Hell, I forgot to write down those guys' names. Not exactly my finest hour as a journalist, eh?

What would have been the point? What were you going to do, file a complaint? About what? They suspected foul play; you politely cooperated; they found nothing and let you go. No harm, no foul. Don't overreact. The system worked.

I guess so. But would it have worked if I'd started running?

A dozen years later, I was dispatched to Grand Rapids to help cover a fatal shooting. A city police officer had pulled over an unarmed man in a residential area for an apparent license plate violation. The driver fled on foot. The officer caught up and the two grappled and tumbled across two yards before the policeman shot the motorist in the back of the head.

At first, I didn't feel any connection between this tragedy and my own roadside encounter. They differed in too many ways, in addition to how they ended. The other driver was black; I am white. He was young and had been drinking; I was middle-aged and sober. He was a Congolese immigrant for whom English was a second language; I am native-born and know the mother tongue—and my rights as a citizen.

Yet a familiar chill crept up my spine as I watched an online compilation of camera footage released by the police department. I found myself pausing and rewinding repeatedly at the moment when the officer initially tries to make the arrest. The driver jerks away, pauses for a split second, then bolts. What was he thinking? I studied his face at that instant, trying to read his expression—a mixture of shock, fear and...something else, it seemed, something I couldn't quite put my finger on.

Was his mind at war with itself, as mine had been? Was he unable to suppress the impulse to flee that I barely had overcome? Was one simple, spur-of-the-moment choice the only thing separating my fate from his? Had the combined weight of our differing circumstances been just enough to tip the scales and trigger opposite responses to our fight-or-flight instincts, so that I walked away unscathed, and he died face down in the grass?

One sultry summer night in eastern North Carolina when I was fifteen or so, a buddy and I ambled through a patch of woods near our blue-collar suburban neighborhood to a clearing where a house was under construction. Someone had set, and abandoned, a small fire in a shallow pit nearby. We kicked a few pieces of scrap lumber onto the smoldering coals and watched them burn, as boys will do.

A carport light came on at a house across a field. A man emerged, looked our way, and went back inside. A few minutes later we heard a siren in the distance. Only when the sound got nearer did we realize—they were coming for *us!*

We tore through the trees, dove into a ditch when a sheriff's car rushed by shining a spotlight here and there, and slipped into my house gasping for breath. A few minutes later came a knock at the front door. A deputy told my father they were looking for the people who had set a fire at the construction site! My pal and I, watching television in the adjacent room, sat frozen. Fortunately, Dad knew nothing about what we'd been up to, and the officer left.

Why had we run? We hadn't done anything really wrong; the little fire posed no danger and we hadn't even started it. But I recall terror coursing through my body as we fled. They'd never believe us. They'd charge us with trespassing or arson or who knew what. We'd be jailed and my family disgraced.

With a half-century's hindsight, I can't quarrel too much with my youthful self's choice. I still have doubts that we'd have gotten a fair shake from the deputy. Sure was a hell of a risk, though, because you know what he'd have asked if he'd caught us: *Why did you run if you were innocent?*

"Headlong flight—wherever it occurs—is the consummate act of evasion: it is not necessarily indicative of wrongdoing, but it is certainly suggestive of such," the U.S. Supreme Court decreed in a 2000 opinion. It affirmed police authority to stop and search people who hightail it after spotting officers on the street, if there's some justifiable reason to suspect wrongdoing. What's justifiable is, apparently, open to interpretation.

The last time I drove through the Upper Peninsula, a song on the radio reminded me of the night I was pulled over on highway 77. Kenny Rogers, giving voice to a dying gambler's saloon wisdom: You gotta know when to hold 'em, fold 'em, walk away or run. Streetwise advice for playing the game called life. I smiled ruefully, even sang along.

Huck Finn would appreciate this little ballad. He might have been short on book learning, but damned if the kid didn't have a keen instinct for wriggling out of sticky situations. When gun-toting bad guys chasing runaway slaves approached the river raft where Jim was hiding, Huck bluffed them away with a clever ruse about smallpox. Later, threatened with lynching alongside the con-artist king and duke—which he probably couldn't talk his way out of—he took to his heels.

Do I have Huck's talent for self-preservation? Hard to say, because I've seldom needed it. I didn't have to repeatedly outsmart or outrun an abusive, alcoholic father and spend my childhood scrounging for scraps and sleeping in barrels. Nor have I attempted anything as risky as helping a wronged fugitive escape to freedom... yet. And of course, I've never been in Jim's position, or anywhere close to it.

But we live in strange, dangerous times. Nowadays I find myself pondering whether my future holds more scares like the roadside pullover and the construction site fire, more on-the-spot choices that could save my neck. Or not. The gambling parable in Kenny's song suddenly has wider resonance for people like me. People whose privileged status in society has made us confident that the legal system is mostly honest, that the dealer at our table isn't playing with a stacked deck.

The casino has new management, corrupt and malevolent. The rules are whatever the boss decides. The stakes are higher: be careful what you report, journalists, or what you tell your classes, teachers, if you value your jobs. Pull those books off the shelves, librarians, if you want your doors to stay open. Shut up about climate change, scientists, or bye-bye to your funding. The targets aren't just people of color, gays and immigrants anymore. How about that?

Lots of us who previously had little cause to fear the flashing lights or the knock at the door may have to weigh our odds as the autocracy spreads its tentacles. Do we cash in our chips and sit the whole thing out? Many, perhaps most, will go along to get along — do their jobs, drive the kids to soccer practice, take that retirement trip to Europe — and do fine, as long as they don't make waves and the economy stays afloat. Or do we decide that we must remain at the table because this isn't a game at all but a fight for the soul of a nation? Speak out, attend protests? Even take it up a notch and risk arrest — help the pregnant woman cross state lines for an abortion, blow the whistle on an impending ICE raid? Get in "good trouble," as John Lewis called it?

Those who play at that level will need a potent mix of the gambler's judgment and Huck's guile, and maybe even his quick feet. Know when to hold, fold, walk away — or fly like the wind. I can still run, by the way, even in my seventh decade. Pretty fast and far for my age. But better yet to stand, isn't it? Stand with others. Stand alone if necessary. Just stand.

Phillip Sterling
THE MIRACLE OF HIGHER ELEVATIONS

Here things happen without rhyme or reason. Trees cluster to stay warm, the sky a vibrant hive. There is much loss. And what is lost is lost to snow the color of a saddle blanket on a dingy, arthritic horse. Night arrives early, outstays its welcome. Things disappear in thin air—breath and love alike.

And for all this snow bares its soul in the usual places. Light trips fantastic. Soon there will be queens enough. Soon the sweet tidings of majesty will buzz and hum.

Ryan McCarty
NEVER ASKING

My mom was one of those who shivered in
the bedroom facing the wind. Us kids,
tucked deep in the back, never asked why
she slept balled up there, buried like an acorn
waiting out the freeze, under the leaves, rooting
down in those nightly drafts, dipping her toes
in that cold, or why only one gas clunker
heated the whole place anyway. We'd just flop
along the blower vent, soaking in the warm until
our skin flaked and my mom's frigid fingers
would rake the itch away. We were between
her and the warmth, but she swayed like branches
full of leaves and sun, never asking if we knew
how winter burned, or when the cold would end.

Patricia Clark
ONE SISTER SAID TO THE OTHER "I HAVE SAD NEWS"

The path I take in the mornings is flat stones,
set in grass, schist or chert, I never got the name
right. This morning, snow and ice. Then streaks
of blood. Something moving, north, on the wing,
hoping to avoid its fate. I stoop down, touch.

Beyond my lookout hut is all a Breughel landscape,
brown trees and snow, a meadow where our neighbor
builds a fire, a portable gray shed, and a group of tree
rounds, circled, he uses with his kids to sit on
or chop wood. The creek is a diagonal slash.

If you stood here with me long enough, I'd tell
the tale of trees—how one crashed down in wind,
barely missing me, how another was pulled down
by a crew, incompetent, right on top
of a favorite living red bud. And there's more.

She told me what went down. One more loss
for her in a series, and we spoke on the phone of building
a tale to fit them into: a grief untold, the day
the two of them brought her home from the breeder,
the name Dave gave her, and now he's dead,

and so is she, poor pup. There are questions I never ask,
and later, wonder why my sister waited a week
to tell me. She says it all with a steady voice,
the reason why, I know. What I don't ever ask,
and she refuses to say, hangs in winter air.

Monica Rico
AUTOPILOT

I am wearing my sandals in November. My love
language is fire, is lake, is whitefish.
I don't want to do
what I have to do
tomorrow. I am in a place
no one wants to be in.
Sometimes I believe

the nurses are being sentenced.
One had to leave dialysis because
she was afraid she'd get air in the veins.
This is funny.

It doesn't matter
if we die
because we have
been defined
as statistically, close.

I no longer feel strange
naked, after a surgeon put her
fingers in my lungs.

Tonight I will sleep in my bathing suit.
I go to anchor in the morning. My husband
tells me I'm not alone. In the city,
I have to twinkle the blue lights.
No screech owls—just a strip club down stairs.
I don't know why the nurse offers me water.
She never brings it unlike my husband
who kisses my forehead each time.

He watches them see me naked. He turns around
to remind me, I am human to him—
not a list of yes and no.
He isn't surprised I'm alive.
He expects it.
Less daunting we are,
naked. Sails down. Lines neatly coiled.

Julia Bedell
TO BE ONE OF THE BIRDS

Meg heard the party from across the street before she got to Paul's house. She hadn't seen him since spring, when they spent a night together after meeting on an app. She paused before opening the door and clutched her tote bag containing a six-pack of beer.

Paul grew up here, in Anchorage, and seemed to enjoy playing host. He spent summers in the Arctic documenting migratory bird populations. In May, right before he left, he had invited Meg over for dinner on what she considered their third date.
Now it was the end of August, and Paul was back in town. Meg hadn't heard from him since he left. So when she got his text—an impersonal invitation to an end of summer party—she surprised herself by attending.

annual backyard bacchanal
byo booze, buddies, birthday suit

Meg opened the door and hoped for a familiar face. It had been naive to arrive alone and expect to know someone. The living room furniture was pushed against the wall and a dozen or so strangers stood around a large table in the kitchen, busy with conversation. The light hit a mobile made of tiny skulls that Paul collected on his research trips. Meg remembered thinking it was beautiful, how he made art out of bird skeletons, when he showed it to her.

Meg walked to the back of the kitchen, placed her beer on the counter, and opened the fridge. It was full of beverages, as well as sausages and large bowls filled with what could be salad. She saw chocolate milk in the side door and remembered how Paul told her he had recently rediscovered his love of it. She remembered how he had offered her some, its taste nostalgic and sweet.

"Probably not worth trying to fit anything in there." Meg turned, her hand holding open the refrigerator door. The woman who had spoken was reaching for a cup in a cabinet. Meg watched as she moved a mug to the side and felt further back until she smiled and pulled out a metal pint glass. Meg glimpsed the word *ornithology* before the woman turned and filled the cup with water from the sink.

"Thanks," Meg said. "Good point." She closed the door. "Um. Are you Paul's housemate?"

"Oh, no." The woman smiled and turned off the tap. "Just a bit too comfortable rummaging through the kitchen." She laughed. "Sorry," she said. "I'm Fiona. An old friend."

Meg observed her. Fiona's skin was tan and everything about her seemed elegant, from the way her hand wrapped loosely around the metal cup to her high cheekbones and silver hoops running up one ear. Her hair was dark and fell out of a loose bun. Meg was pleased to notice a few gray strands along Fiona's part, then felt embarrassed for seeking her flaws.

"I'm Meg. A newish acquaintance, I guess."

"Welcome! Always nice to get new people around here," Fiona said. "Otherwise, it's just the same high school party on repeat."

"Thanks. Sounds like, um, a big party," Meg said.

"Ha, it's all right." Fiona looked at the six-pack Meg was still holding. "Can I offer you a drink? There are coolers out back if you want to store your beer there, and there's also a bunch of mixers and things."

"Sure," Meg said. "I'll have what you do."

Fiona smiled. "You might not want that. I'm mostly sober now."

Meg suddenly felt silly holding her six IPAs.

"But just because I'm boring doesn't mean you should be! Why don't I make you something? It'll be fun," Fiona said.

Meg nodded and watched Fiona take a plastic cup from a bag on the counter instead of getting another glass from the cabinet. Fiona filled it with ice, a splash of gin, some soda, and limes.

"This used to be my favorite," she said and handed it to Meg.

Meg took a sip and her tongue lit up with sour effervescence. "Whoa. That's good."

Fiona smiled and Meg could tell she was one of those people with a symmetrical face, the ones you can't help but notice. She wondered how often Fiona had sat at the kitchen table and watched Paul cook. She wondered if Paul had mentioned her and if it was obvious she was here because she'd slept with him.

The door to the backyard opened and a man walked in. He smiled when he saw Fiona. Neither Fiona nor the man seemed to notice Meg. She took another sip of her drink and looked around the room, but everyone still seemed occupied. Not wanting to hover, she slipped past Fiona's friend and opened the back door.

Paul's yard extended to a forested area along the creek. The sun was below the trees, and it was beginning to get dark. Two fire pits illuminated the crowd, one closer to the back deck and one along the edge of the woods. Meg sipped her drink and walked onto the grass, its chill reaching her feet through her sandals. She stood near the closer fire and watched people play horseshoes.

"Hey," a man about Meg's height was standing on the other side of the fire pit. He had curly brown hair and was wearing a tie-dyed sweatshirt.

"Hi," Meg said.

"You look familiar. I think we met at that photo walk the other week?"

"Oh, yeah," Meg said. "I was there." She sipped her drink again.

The guy asked Meg about herself, and she relaxed as they chatted. Through the dimming light, her eye caught two tall and slender figures walking across the yard. One of them stopped by the other fire pit and pushed back his hair. It was Paul. He'd grown a mullet since the last time she saw him. Meg watched him light a cigarette and take a drag. She wondered if she should go say hi.

The other figure had Fiona's messy bun and black cutoff shorts. Fiona turned to face Paul and held up a cigarette. Meg watched Fiona place the unlit cigarette in her mouth as Paul brought his toward her. Fiona inhaled and a flame pulsed between them. Paul remained close to Fiona until she stepped back and released smoke into the air.

Meg shivered. She felt shaky, almost feverish, as if the fire next to her had gone out. The man who'd been talking to her looked concerned. "Want my sweatshirt?" he asked.

Meg shook her head. "No, thanks. I just need to go inside for a minute."

"Oh. I can come with you!"

"No, I'm okay." Meg's feet felt frozen as she walked across the lawn.

"Wait, what's your name?" The man said from behind her.

"Meg."

"Oh, cool. I'm Gary!"

Meg walked up the back steps and into the kitchen, then turned left down a hallway. The bathroom was the farthest on the right, past Paul's room. She closed the bathroom door behind her and sat on the toilet. Despite having to go, it took a moment before her body relaxed.

When she left the bathroom, she hovered near Paul's bedroom door. It was open, and she could see the chair pushed against his desk. She remembered their night together. He had cooked her king salmon, the best kind of fish. It was the last of his filets from the previous summer and the first time Meg had eaten it. The entire meal was delicious. Meg sat at the kitchen table and watched him chop and roast vegetables while telling her about growing up a few miles away.

He told her about the time when he was in elementary school and took the trash out to the street on a dark winter morning only to run into a gigantic bull moose. They would sometimes ski to school, he said, and he'd try to keep up with his sister as she practiced her pole plants and glides. Meg thought of her own childhood in suburban Ohio. Paul's life was what she dreamed of when she moved to Alaska. In his kitchen, she confirmed it was real.

After they ate, he offered for her to spend the night. She agreed, and it was nice. She was surprised by how affectionate he was. While dozing off, she felt him press into her hair. "You smell good," she remembered him murmuring.

The next morning, Meg woke up to find Paul quietly dressing himself. He looked embarrassed to see her awake. He told her he'd forgotten about needing to drive his nephew to a doctor's appointment, but that he'd had a nice time. She could help herself to coffee if she wanted before she left. Then he waved his wrist in a half-hearted goodbye and slipped out the door.

Meg remembered lying in his bed and feeling happy despite the abrupt end. She had waited for him to ask her on another date. After three days he did but then canceled it. He said he was overwhelmed with preparing for his fieldwork. They didn't see each other again before he left.

Walking further into Paul's room, Meg recognized the photo of him and his sister taped to his mirror. They were younger and blonder and cute and smiling. Meg remembered how she'd asked him who was in the photo and, when he told her, it made her like him more. She couldn't imagine her brother having a photo of her in his room. Then again, she wouldn't know if he did.

Meg heard a noise in the kitchen and froze before peering down the hallway. She did not want to be caught here. But the hall was empty, so she walked quietly back to the kitchen. Her six-pack was on the counter with two beers removed. She took a third one, opened it, and went back outside.

Paul and Fiona were still standing by the fire pit. Meg headed down the steps and across the yard toward them.

"Hey, Fiona," Meg said, while glancing at Paul.

"Hi there." Fiona smiled and Paul shifted from one foot to another.

"Hey," he said to Meg. "Glad you came."

"Thanks," Meg said. She felt herself wanting to make him jealous. "Fiona, that drink was so good."

"Aw, good. In retrospect I should've had one with you, now I'm stuck with Paul's beer."

Meg noted the can in Fiona's hand.

"I didn't mean to pressure you," Paul said.

Fiona laughed and took another sip. "I need something to warm me before the swim."

Paul scanned the yard. It was dark and people crowded around the fires as sparks flew up in the sky.

"Yeah," Paul said. "I think it's time."

Meg took a gulp of her beer. She felt childlike, not only because she was a good deal shorter than both Paul and Fiona but also because she was trying to catch onto a coded conversation.

"What do you mean by swim?" Meg said.

"It's tradition," Fiona said. "The goodbye-to-summer plunge before the dark takes us."

"We've done it for years now," Paul said. "Here, let's go."

Fiona and Meg trailed Paul as he walked to the guy who'd been running the sound system on the deck. After Paul whispered in his ear, the man hit pause on the music and yelled: "To the creek!" The party stopped and everyone began down the root-covered path in the woods at the back of Paul's yard.

Meg tried to keep close to Paul and Fiona but at one point she lost her footing and had to stop. When she looked up, they were far ahead and followed by a group of people. She wondered if she should go back to the house or go home.

"Hey, Meg," someone said, and she felt a hand on her shoulder. Meg recognized the guy in the tie dye from earlier. Gary. It took her a minute to remember his name.

"Hi!" Meg said, grateful. "Are you going swimming?" She felt silly after saying that. Presumably everyone on this path was going swimming.

"Only if you are," he said. Meg didn't respond. Gary paused, then said, "Sorry, I mean, that was a joke. You should do whatever makes you comfortable. But yeah, I'm gonna!"

Meg smiled in the dark. "Thanks," she said. "Yeah, I'll go."

"Excellent," Gary said, and smiled. They continued along until they reached the creek. The water was calm, and someone had arranged rocks to make standing pools for dipping. Meg watched as people stripped off their clothes and threw themselves in with yelps as they touched the cold water. She glanced around for Paul.

She saw him on the bank, shirtless, watching. Meg followed his gaze to see Fiona dunk her head before surfacing, gasping, her dark hair slick against her head. Her statuesque body glistened in the ambient light that filtered through the trees.

Meg's heart sank. This person was impossibly beautiful. More than that, she appeared designed to exist here as if her body was made from this river and these woods.

Meg watched Fiona get out of the water and stand next to Paul, wringing her hair. She watched as he gave her his shirt to dry off with, then put on her shorts and sweatshirt. She watched as Paul said something to Fiona, and they wandered along the river away from the party.

"Hey, Meg," someone said. Meg turned to see Gary waving to her from the next pool over. She looked behind her again, but the woods were dark, Paul and Fiona out of sight.

Fiona's image hung in Meg's mind, barely punctuated by the sight of others jumping in as well. How would it feel to be one of them? To have her body glisten and, perhaps, have someone gaze at her the way she had just gazed? Meg walked toward her new friend as if pulled by gravity. She stood at the edge of the water, took a deep breath, and began to remove her clothes.

The water was bracing. Meg dunked her head and felt needles stab her skin. The pain seemed necessary. It had felt so good to be in Paul's orbit. To sit at the table and eat the food and visualize the stories from a wild land. He opened a door and for a moment, she was inside the life she sought.

Meg emerged and the air felt nearly warm. She saw Gary watch her and wondered if she inspired the same image as she'd just seen. But Meg was not long and lean. She had thick legs, a butt, and the regular amount of flab for girls in their twenties. A different kind of statue.

Meg smiled as Gary averted his eyes from her body. He handed her a towel.

"Where did you get this?" Meg said while wrapping the warm fabric around her.

"It's not my first of these parties," Gary said. "I've learned some tricks."

Meg felt herself warming. "How do you know these guys?"

"I mean, at a certain point Anchorage gets small. But I used to work with Gavin." Meg's face was blank, and Gary nodded.

"Paul's housemate, the guy playing music earlier."

"Oh. Cool."

"And you?" Gary said.

"Hm." Meg wasn't sure how she wanted to answer. She began to put on her clothes and regretted not having socks. She was warm now except for her feet.

"Paul dates a lot of girls," Gary said. "It's okay, I mean, if that's why you're here."

Meg shivered. She was suddenly cold again. Maybe it had been very dumb to do this.

"I need to go back to the house," she said.

Gary nodded. "Okay."

Gary trailed Meg in silence. When they reached the first fire pit, which only had a few people around it, he touched her arm.

"Listen, I didn't mean to offend you. By saying that about Paul and you earlier."

Meg felt something happening in her chest and feared she might start to cry. She shook her head. "Don't be sorry," she said. "I just, um, need to use the bathroom."

She handed him the towel and walked across the yard and inside, not bothering to look around. She entered the bathroom and noticed on her way that the door to Paul's room was closed. How foolish to think she'd meant anything to him.

Meg lingered in the bathroom and let the tap run until she heard a knock on the door. She stopped the water, toweled off her face, and attempted to make her damp hair presentable before opening the door with a forced smile.

Fiona stood outside. Her face was strained, so unlike the elegant ease Meg saw earlier. As Fiona registered Meg she attempted to regain her composure. But the look Meg had seen was somewhere between grief and despair.

"Oh, hi," Meg said. Fiona looked down and slid through the doorway past Meg.

"Sorry, I just need," she said, and closed the door.

Meg lingered in the hallway. Minutes later, the bathroom door was still closed. She thought about knocking to check on Fiona, then turned and slowly walked outside. People were gathered by the fire pits again, and a group had started dancing around the closer one. Meg wondered what happened with Paul and Fiona in the woods. She assessed the yard but didn't see him.

Just as she was about to leave, a familiar figure emerged from the forest. He appeared to sway, and his face seemed oddly serene. Meg watched as he wandered over to the dancers. She watched him approach a young-looking blond woman wearing only a tank top and shorts. She watched as he put his hands on her waist and danced closely against her. The woman turned to face him, and Meg couldn't see her expression. Paul pressed his face into hers.

Meg walked inside. The overhead lights were off, and the kitchen was dark save for one lamp above the oven. The mobile's tiny bird skulls appeared ghoulish in the glow. Meg watched them turn, their eye sockets black and their cheekbones impossibly high and illuminated. She was ready, now, to go.

Sheena M. Carey
KINTSUGI

Golden threads bind cracked shards together
Cracked shards because life happens haphazardly
Cracked shards because choices taken ill-considered
Cracked shards because, just because

Silver tendrils hold the broken parts together
Broken parts because life happens dangerously
Broken parts because choices can be woefully wrong
Broken parts because, just because

Platinum strands meld the jagged edges together
Jagged edges because life can happen with sharpness
Jagged edges because choices can cut in strange directions
Jagged edges because, just because

Making something unified with precious binding, because
Making something whole out of the brokenness, because
Making something stronger through resilience, because
Making something beautiful in the creation, because

Cracked shards,
Broken parts,
Jagged edges,
Kintsugi. Just because.

Russ Capaldi
LIGHTER THINGS

Once in June years ago,
in our truck exploring
a cedar swamp —
so far back we found
a shaded two-track
that still had snow,
soft and slick.
So we took out skis
and skied on it
back and forth
for half the day —
the best
of two worlds:
gliding back and forth
laughing, lightly clothed,
yellow cowslips on the sides,
through swirls
of insects, as sheer
and quick as
these bright, cold flakes
that fall tonight
as I shovel the driveway's drifts;
and the sharp, sweet scent of cedar
from the neighbor's woodpile,
and there! the scent
of deep black earth —
from where this time of year?
What foundation,
made of lighter things,
did we unwittingly lay
in ourselves back then,
together yes, but individually?

Over the years she's sent
me postcards from where
she's been; brief and fancy-free.
But if one comes tomorrow
I wish it would start
last night I caught
the scent of something
on the air.

Devin Wilson
CRICKETS

in the distance.
Thunder and light
rain. Cows return
to pasture. A child
rides by and waves.
The lawnmower stalls,
a dog barks. Chickadee
and warbler songs.
Motorcycles, fireworks,
the no-sound of grass
growing, July oozing
down the valley
of my mouth.

CONTRIBUTOR BIOS

DEBORAH ALLBRITAIN is the author of *Osgood* (Brick Road Poetry Press, 2024). Her work appears in *Ploughshares, Ecotone, Beloit Poetry Journal,* and *Verse Daily*. She won the Patricia Dobler Poetry Prize and has been nominated for the Pushcart Prize and Best of the Net. More at willaflora.com.

* **COLLEEN ALLES** is a native Michigander and award-winning writer living in Grand Rapids. The author of three novels and two poetry collections, she's also a fiction editor with Barren Magazine and an MFA candidate at Spalding University. You can find her online at www.colleenalles.com.

JULIA BEDELL grew up in Brooklyn and now lives in Alaska. Her fiction reflects her engagement with urban and rural landscapes, as well as her desire to use place and setting to reveal emotional narrative. You can find her published work at juliabedell.tumblr.com.

SHEENA M. CAREY has been writing poetry for performance and on commission for nearly 40 years for collaborations including the Coyaba Dance Theater in Washington, DC. and Milwaukee's Ko-Thi Dance Company. Recent work includes original poems for Marquette University's 2024 Ignatian Retreat on Race Relations. She is Internship Director and Lecturer for the Marquette University Diederich College of Communication.

* **PATRICIA CLARK** is the author of *O Lucky Day* (Madville, 2025) and *Self-Portrait with a Million Dollars*. A poem from *O Lucky Day* ("What My Father Wished For") won a Pushcart Prize and will be published in the 2026 Pushcart Anthology vol L. Recent work appears in *Plume, Sheila-na-Gig,* and *Cimarron Review*.

* **ANDREW COLLARD** is the author of *Sprawl* (Ohio University Press, 2023) and winner of the Hollis Summers Poetry Prize. His poems have appeared in *Ploughshares, AGNI, Kenyon Review,* and elsewhere. He lives with his son in Grand Rapids, MI.

* **SHUTTA CRUM** is a Robinson Jeffers Tor House honoree (2024) and recipient of nine Royal Palm Literary Awards (FL). Her poems have appeared in many journals. A Pushcart nominee, she has three chapbooks in print, three novels, and fifteen children's books. She publishes the newsletter The Wordsmith's Playground. www.shutta.com

ROGER D'AGOSTIN is a writer living in Connecticut. His work has appeared in *Bridge Eight, Five South, StoryBottle Co.*, as well as many other literary journals.

❋ **ROBERT FANNING** is the author of five full-length poetry collections: *All We Are Given We Cannot Hold*, *Severance*, *Our Sudden Museum*, *American Prophet* and *The Seed Thieves*, and three chapbooks: *Prince of the Air*, *Sheet Music*, and *Old Bright Wheel*. He is a Professor at Central Michigan University.

MONICA FINGER is a poet and musician residing in Buffalo, New York. Her drumming, lyrics, and vocals are featured on the album *Event* by Enemy of the Rose. Her writing explores grief, apostasy, and transgressive desire, and has been featured by the Just Buffalo Literary Center and others.

❋ **JOHN FLESHER** is a retired Associated Press reporter and was inducted into the Michigan Journalism Hall of Fame in 2025. His literary essays have appeared in *Dunes Review*, *Bear River Review*, and *Transformational*. A longtime resident of Traverse City, Michigan, he now lives in Raleigh, North Carolina.

❋ **TYLER FRANZ** is a photographer based in Traverse City, Michigan, focused on weddings, portraits, families, music, animals, and senior portraits. Although these are his main pursuits, he is available to shoot photographs of any kind.

❋ **DAN GERBER** took his vows to "see the world through words and letters and to see words and letter through the world" on August 20, 1962. He has published novels, volumes of short stories, non-fiction, and ten volumes of poems.

❋ **MARY JO FIRTH GILLETT's** collection, *Soluble Fish*, won the Crab Orchard First Book Contest. She has four award-winning chapbooks and her poems have appeared in *The Southern Review*, *New Ohio Review*, *Plant-Human Quarterly*, *Dunes Review*, *Southern Poetry Review*, *Harvard Review*, *Third Coast*, *Florida Review*, *Poetry Daily*, *Verse Daily*, and elsewhere.

❋ **ALICE HAINES's** poems have appeared in *Does It Have Pockets*, *The Healing Muse*, *Northern New England Review*, *Off the Coast*, *Pangyrus LitMag*, *Pine Row*, and *Touchstone Literary Magazine*. A retired family physician who lives in Maine, she volunteers at a free clinic and enjoys native plants, birding, and tracking.

❋ **DAVID HARDIN** is the author of the 2021 memoir, *Standpipe: Delivering Water In Flint* (Belt), a 2022 Michigan Notable Book; the 2020 poetry book, *Dreaming Bob Wills* (Silverbow); and the forthcoming memoir, *Water Finds A Way* (Cornerstone). His work has appeared in *Dunes Review* and *Michigan Quarterly Review*.

❋ **CLAIRE HELAKOSKI** is a writer and educator living in Hancock, Michigan. Her nonfiction has recently appeared in *OxMag* and *South Florida Poetry Review*. Her poetry has recently appeared in *Thirteen Bridges Review* and *Panoply*. She lives with her husband, two children, and goldendoodle.

RICHARD HOFFMAN's nine books include the Massachusetts Book Award–winning poetry collection *Noon until Night*, and the recent *People Once Real*. He is Emeritus Writer-in-Residence at Emerson College and nonfiction editor of *Solstice: A Magazine of Diverse Voices*.

※ **ANITA HUNT** is a poet and retired adjunct English professor from Cadillac, Michigan, who writes about nature and life in northern Michigan and southwestern Montana. She and her husband live in an old farmhouse full of pet fur, grandchildren's artwork, and the messy evidence of myriad artistic and historical pursuits.

※ Born and raised on the third coast, **DAVID JAMES** has published nine books and has had over thirty of his one-act plays produced in the U.S., Ireland, and England.

※ **ANDREW JETER** teaches writing, research, and film. He holds a PhD in English Composition & Applied Linguistics. His poems have been published by *Silver Birch Press*, *Panoply*, and *Peninsula Poets*. His first collection of poetry is *Ancient Memories*.

※ **JEFF KASS** is the author of *Knuckleheads*, the Independent Publishers Best Short Fiction Collection of 2011; and three full-length poetry collections, including *Teacher/Pizza Guy*, a 2020 Michigan Notable Book. His newest poetry collection, *True Believer*, consists of poems that spin around and through Marvel Comics and the Marvel Cinematic Universe.

※ **ELIZABETH KERLIKOWSKE** helps manage the Kalamazoo Writers Disorganization. She is currently part of Ripple Effect, a collaboration between musicians, poets, and the Kalamazoo Valley Museum. She will be teaching an ekphrastic workshop in the fall of 2025 at the Kalamazoo Institute of Arts.

MARY DEAN LEE's debut collection *Tidal* (April 2024) was shortlisted for Quebec Writer's Federation Poetry Prize. New poems are out or forthcoming in *Hamilton Stone Review*, *Free State Review*, and *MicroLit*. She grew up in Georgia and received her PhD in organizational behavior at Yale. She lives in Montreal.

MICHAEL MARK is the author of *Visiting Her in Queens is More Enlightening than a Month in a Monastery in Tibet* which won the 2022 Rattle Chapbook Prize. His work appears in several journals and *The Best New Poets*, 2024. His poem "Devotion" received a Pushcart Prize, 2026. michaeljmark.com

* **RYAN MCCARTY** is a writer and teacher living in Ypsilanti, MI. Since his beard started greying, his writing started getting published in places like *Coal City Review, Collateral, Door is a Jar, Hamilton Stone Review, One Art, Rattle,* and *Trailer Park Quarterly.*

KARA PENN lives in Denver, Colorado, with her husband, four daughters, and two spirited puppies. Her work has appeared in *The Threepenny Review, Studies in Arts and Humanities Journal, The Pickled Body,* and *Meadowlands Review.* She writes in the spaces between mothering, running a small business, and daily life's messy beauty.

* **LEANN PETERSON** lives in Grand Rapids, MI. She enjoys writing stories about people, places, and things that are close to her heart. Currently, LeAnn is working on a memoir about her brother Tim.

MONICA RICO works as a scientific contributor in the effort to eradicate cancer. When she is not in hospitals, she applies her scholarship to nutrition, social biology, and Madonna. She is the author of the poetry collection, *Pinion.*

* **NANCY SQUIRES'** writing has appeared in *Dunes Review, Blueline Magazine, Split Rock Review,* and Writers Resist. In 2014, she self-published a memoir, *The Cottage: Portrait of a Place,* set on the shores of Grand Traverse Bay. She lives in Michigan with her partner and two cats.

MEGHAN STERLING (she/her/hers) is a writer and working mother living in Maine. Her collections include *View from a Borrowed Field,* which won Lily Poetry Review's Paul Nemser Book Prize, and *You Are Here to Break Apart* (Lily Poetry Review Press). *Sick Poems from the Lovebed* (Harbor Editions) is forthcoming in 2026.

* **PHILLIP STERLING's** most recent book is *Lessons in Geography: The Education of a Michigan Poet,* a collection of essays and memoir (Cornerstone, 2024).

* **KEITH TAYLOR's** most recent book, *What Can the Matter Be?* (Wayne State University Press, 2024), was chosen by the Library of Michigan as a 2025 Michigan Notable Book. In 2024, he also published *All the Time You Want: Selected Poems, 1977–2017* with Dzanc Books.

* **KARLY VANCE** grew up in Bay City, Michigan, and studied writing at Hope College. Her writing has been published in journals including *Midwest Quarterly, Madison Review,* and *Flying Island Review.* She lives with her family in the Chicago area.

B. A. VAN SISE is an author and photographic artist with three monographs: *Children of Grass* with Mary-Louise Parker, *Invited to Life* with Mayim Bialik, and *On the National Language* with DeLanna Studi. His awards include the Lascaux Prize for Nonfiction and the Independent Book Publishers Awards gold medal, twice.

* **ELLEN STONE** advises a poetry club at Ann Arbor's Community High School, co-hosts an online monthly poetry series, Skazat!, and is an editor at Public School Poetry. Her most recent collection is *Everybody Wants to Keep the Moon Inside Them* (Mayapple Press, 2025).

* **JASON GORDY WALKER's** poems and book reviews appear or are forthcoming in *Asymptote, Birmingham Poetry Review, Louisiana Literature, Nimrod International Journal, Pembroke Magazine*, and others, and his translations of poems from the Norwegian of Rune Christiansen are forthcoming at *B O D Y* (Czech Republic) and *Cordite Poetry Review* (Australia).

* Author and poet **JULIE BONNER WILLIAMS** lives with her husband on the southwest shores of Lake Michigan. A former English professor, she now writes full-time. Her essays and articles have been featured in *Michigan Blue* magazine, *Grand Rapids Magazine*, and other publications. Her first book was recently bought by Arcadia Publishing.

DEVIN WILSON is a poet based in coastal Maine. His poetry has appeared in or is forthcoming in *Salt Hill Journal, Dunes Review, Humana Obscura, MacQueen's Quinterly* and other literary journals. He studied at Kenyon College and American University and has worked as a journalist, magazine editor, and marketing executive.

KENTON K. YEE's recent poems appear in *Kenyon Review, Threepenny Review, Cincinnati Review, RHINO, Quarterly West, Poetry Northwest, Constellations, Denver Quarterly, Terrain.org, DIAGRAM, Attached to the Living World: A New Ecopoetry Anthology, I-70 Review, Rattle*, and other venues. He writes from Northern California. FB: @scrambled.k.eggs INSTA: @kentonkyeepoet

APRIL YU is a teenage writer from New Jersey. Her work has been recognized by *The New York Times*, Scholastic Art and Writing Awards, Wigleaf Top 50, and Ringling College of Art and Design. She is a graduate of the Adroit Summer Mentorship Program and Kenyon Young Writers Workshop.

* denotes Michigan native or resident

STAFF BIOS

*KELLI FITZPATRICK is an author, editor, and teacher from Michigan. Her first novel, *Captain Marvel: Carol Danvers Declassified*, is available from BenBella Books. Her short fiction has been published by Simon and Schuster, Baen Books, Flash Fiction Online, and others. She holds an MFA in Creative Writing from Iowa State University. Website: KelliFitzpatrick.com

*CHRIS GIROUX received his doctorate from Wayne State University and is a professor of English at Saginaw Valley State University, where he has served as faculty advisor for the school's literary magazine and co-founded the community arts journal *Still Life*. His second chapbook, *Sheltered in Place*, was released in 2022.

*ANNE-MARIE OOMEN is Michigan Author for 2023-24. Her memoir, *As Long As I Know You: The Mom Book* won AWP's Sue William Silverman Nonfiction Award. She wrote *Lake Michigan Mermaid* with Linda Nemec Foster, *Love, Sex and 4-H* (Next Generation Indie Award/Memoir), and others. *The Lake Huron Mermaid* is most recent, now out.

*JOHN MAUK has published a range of stories and nonfiction works, including his full collections, *Field Notes for the Earthbound* and *Where All Things Flatten*. John also hosts Prose from the Underground, a YouTube video series for working writers. For more information, see johnmauk.com.

*SARA MAURER lives with her family in Michigan's Upper Peninsula. She honed her creative writing craft while completing Stanford's Continuing Studies Novel Writing Certificate program. Her debut novel, *A Good Animal*, is coming February 24, 2026 from St. Martin's Press. Find her at www.saramaurerwrites.com.

*TERESA SCOLLON's fourth poetry collection, *No Trouble Staying Awake*, is now out from Cornerstone Press. A National Endowment for the Arts fellow, she teaches the Writers Studio program at North Ed Career Tech in Traverse City.

*YVONNE STEPHENS is a poet, rural librarian, amateur mycologist and mental health activist. *The Salt Before It Shakes* was published by Hidden Timber Books in 2017. Her work has appeared in *Dunes Review, Family Stories from the Attic, Eucalypt,* and *io Literary Journal*.

*JENNIFER YEATTS' literary life has included MA and MFA degrees in poetry, teaching writing in various forms, a handful of small publications, and editorial roles at *Passages North* and *Fugue*. For money, she teaches people about coffee and Pilates.

NATIONAL WRITERS SERIES
A Year-Round Book Festival

CELEBRATING 15 YEARS OF EXCEPTIONAL AUTHORS, EXTRAORDINARY CONVERSATIONS!

LOOK WHO'S BEEN HERE...

Mitch Albom, David Sedaris, Margaret Atwood, Jason Reynolds, Alice Walker, Tom Brokaw, Pete Souza, Ann Patchett, Amy Tan, Fredrik Backman, Jeannette Walls, Anna Quindlen, Diane Rehm

YOU WON'T BELIEVE WHO'S COMING NEXT!

The National Writers Series of Traverse City is a nonprofit organization dedicated to holding great conversations with today's best authors and building the creative writing skills of youth.

For information on author events, student writing classes, Battle of the Books, college scholarships and more, visit

NationalWritersSeries.com

SUBMISSION GUIDELINES

Dunes Review welcomes work from writers at all stages of their careers living anywhere in the world, though we particularly love featuring those with ties to Michigan and the Midwest. We are open to all styles and aesthetics, but please read the following carefully to dive a little deeper into what we're looking for.

Ultimately, we're looking for work that draws us in from the very first line: with image, with sound, with sense, with lack of sense. We're looking for writing that makes us *feel* and bowls us over, lifts us up, and takes us places we've never been to show us ordinary things in ways we've never seen them. We're looking for poems and stories and essays that teach us how to read them and pull us back to their beginnings as soon as we've read their final lines. We're looking for things we can't wait to read again, things we can't resist sharing with the nearest person who will listen. Send us your best work. We'll give it our best attention.

Submissions are accepted only via our Submittable platform: www.dunesreview.submittable.com. We do not consider work sent through postal mail or email. Any submissions sent through email will not be read or responded to. Please see further guidelines posted on our site. We look forward to reading your work!

Join our community of Michigan Writers!

Annual membership: $50 / Student rate: $20

Membership includes:

- Our monthly email newsletter to stay up to date with events;
- Two annual issues of *Dunes Review*, Northern Michigan's premier literary journal;
- Free admission to Michigan Writers workshops;
- Eligibility for the annual Michigan Writers Cooperative Press chapbook contest;
- And ... well, since we're an organization of members, you decide!

To become a member, visit www.michwriters.org/join

Call for Patrons

What you're reading is pretty special, because the *Dunes Review*:

- Has been continuously published for 28 years
- Is the work of an all-volunteer organization (rather than an educational institution)
- Is still available in print
- Helps newer writers get into print alongside established writers

The cost of publication can be underwritten in part by individual contributions. We invite you to support the publication of the next issue with a donation of $50. Send your check payable to **Michigan Writers** to:

Michigan Writers, P.O. Box 2355

Traverse City, MI 49685

Thank you for your support!

Questions? Contact us at info@michwriters.org.